TITAN

Vinay Kamath is a senior associate editor with *The Hindu BusinessLine* based in Chennai. Prior to joining *BusinessLine* in 1998, he did a short stint in television with TV18, where he was the chief of news bureau, Chennai. He has earlier worked with *Financial Express*, *Business World*, *Times of India* and *Economic Times*. A graduate in economics from Vivekananda College, University of Madras, 1985, Kamath earned a diploma in journalism from the Times School of Journalism, New Delhi, in 1986, and was also a member of the first batch of the Chevening Young Journalists' Fellowship Programme at the University of Westminster, London, in 1995, a scholarship offered by the British Foreign and Commonwealth Office.

Praise for the book

'*Titan* is an intriguing story and could be a lesson to corporations... That the author has captured the nuanced tale with flair and insight certainly makes it a must-read for those keen to follow the journey of Indian titans.' – *Business Today*

'An inspiring story of a successful Indian company that is constantly evolving to keep pace with the times, this book has a lot to offer to management students, start-ups, visionaries who want to make a difference, CEOs and HR heads who wish to build an intrapreneurial culture and marketers.' – *Frontline*

TITAN

INSIDE INDIA'S MOST SUCCESSFUL CONSUMER BRAND

VINAY KAMATH

hachette INDIA

First published in hardback in India in 2018 by Hachette India
(Registered name: Hachette Book Publishing India Pvt. Ltd)
An Hachette UK company
www.hachetteindia.com
This edition published in 2021

SRD

Images on pp. i–xi of photo insert courtesy of B.G. Dwarakanath
Image on p. xi (top) of photo insert courtesy of S. Ravi Kant
All other Images are courtesy of Titan Company Limited

Hardback edition ISBN 978-93-5009-978-0
Paperback edition ISBN 978-93-88322-52-2
Ebook edition ISBN 978-93-5009-979-7

Hachette Book Publishing India Pvt. Ltd
4th & 5th Floors, Corporate Centre
Plot No. 94, Sector 44, Gurugram 122003, India

Typeset in Bembo Std 11/15.5 by
Manmohan Kumar, New Delhi

Printed and bound in India by
by Manipal Technologies Limited, Manipal

MIX
Paper | Supporting responsible forestry
FSC™ C043100

To my parents
Aruna, Malu and Nivi
And to Xerxes Desai, who made Titan what it is today

CONTENTS

Titan's Timeline

August 1975	Xerxes Desai joins Tata Press on return to the Tata Group from secondment to CIDCO.
October 1975	Anil Manchanda joins Tata Press.
Early 1977	Tata Press takes up IAS officer Iravatham Mahadevan's concordance of the Indus script for printing.
16 March 1977	Anil Manchanda visits Mahadevan's office at Udyog Bhavan, New Delhi, to study various sectors wherein the Ministry of Industrial Development would like to see the private sector adopt new projects. Projects range from ophthalmic glass, mechanized fishing boats and granite tombstones to precision engineering including wristwatches.
21 March 1977	Anil calls up Xerxes from Delhi and says that the best project would be to make wristwatches. This is the moment of conception for the Tata Group's foray into watches.
1977–1979	In spite of support from within the Ministry of Industrial Development, the Tata wristwatch project is in the doldrums with no approvals forthcoming from the government.
June 1978	Tata Press attempts to buy Bangalore-based watchmaker Hegde and Golay; makes a small investment in the company, but gives up after a few frustrating months of trying to work with the promoter.
1978	Tamil Nadu Industrial Development Corporation Ltd (TIDCO) establishes contact with France Ebauches SA in its search for a technical collaborator for manufacturing wristwatches as a part of their efforts to establish industries in Tamil Nadu.

September 1979	I. Mahadevan is back in the Tamil Nadu cadre as TIDCO managing director; invites Tata Press to be the joint-venture partner in the project to manufacture watches.
September 1979	Xerxes and Anil visit France Ebauches in Besançon.
1979–1982	Various options are explored with France Ebauches to develop a viable wristwatch project in India. Simultaneous, fruitless, discussions are carried out with the Government of India to see how a Tata-promoted project could find approval.
January 1982	J.R.D. Tata visits France Ebauches.
February 1982	It is decided that Titan will submit a formal application to the government and risk getting a refusal.
March 1982	France Ebauches chief Jacques Perret visits India. Memorandum of understanding signed between Tata Sons and France Ebauches agreeing in principle to participate in a joint venture to manufacture wristwatches.
March 1982	Application submitted by TIDCO to the Government of India for the manufacture of 2 million wristwatches and components with Tata Industries Ltd as co-promoter.
August 1982	Government of India accords approval to TIDCO for the project but the participation of the Tata Group is not permitted as watches are reserved for the small-scale and public sector.
September 1982	In a stunning two-minute meeting the then Secretary of the Ministry of Commerce and Industry tells Minoo Mody, then CEO of Tata Sons, 'Take it from me, Mr Mody, the Tatas will never make watches,' before peremptorily dismissing the Tata team.
March 1983	New investment company, Questar Investments Ltd, is formed with normal capital specifically for 'The Watch Project'.
May 1983	Bhaskar Bhat joins The Watch Project of Tata Press.

February 1984	Agreement signed between TIDCO and Questar to set up a joint sector wristwatch manufacturing company, Titan Watches Ltd.
February 1984	Technical collaboration agreement signed between TIDCO and France Ebauches for The Watch Project and submitted to the Government of India.
July 1984	Titan Watches Ltd incorporated.
1984–85	Location for manufacturing plant identified, project details refined and firmed up.
1 July 1985	I.K. Amitha, retired executive director of HMT Watches, appointed senior vice president (Operations), Titan Watches Ltd.
October 1985	R.C. Hari Rao, M.S. Shantharam and B.G. Dwarakanath join Titan from HMT.
February 1986	B.G. Dwarakanath takes possession of an empty plot of land at Hosur for the Titan factory from SIPCOT, a Tamil Nadu government industrial estates development and promotion body.
March 1986	Ground breaking for watch-manufacturing plant in Hosur.
July 1986	Xerxes, Hari Rao, Shantharam visit France and Switzerland; finalize Swiss plant and machinery for watch assembly and movement parts manufacture.
August 1986	Xerxes, Vibha Paul, Dwarakanath and B.N. Yallamalli visit Hong Kong, Taiwan and Korea to finalize and place orders for appearance parts for watches.
End 1986	Recruitment of first batch of operators for watch assembly.
February 1987	Titan factory commences production.
February 1987	Titan Classique, the first watch made by Titan, ready for commercial release.
March 1987	Titan launches its first set of watches.
March 1987	Titan's path-breaking print and TV advertising campaign released. The signature tune of the campaign still runs with its advertising in 2018,

	probably the longest continuously running advertising feature in Indian advertising.
23 December 1987	Titan opens its first showroom in Bangalore at Safina Plaza, Infantry Road.
11 March 1988	J.R.D. Tata dedicates the Titan factory at a grand function in Hosur.
10 April 1989	Titan crosses the one million watches milestone.
November 1992	Titan ties up with Timex to make and retail watches.
April 1992	Ratan Tata's first visit to Titan.
April 1992	Work is started on the Charles-Correa designed Titan township.
April 1993	Titan forays into Europe with the launch of watches in the United Kingdom.
June 1993	Anil Manchanda quits Titan over differences with Xerxes Desai on the European venture.
19 March 1994	New state-of-the-art jewellery-making facility inaugurated.
25 August 1995	Launch of Titan watches in Europe.
20 July 1996	First Tanishq store inaugurated by actor Suhasini Mani Ratnam on Cathedral Road, Chennai.
April 1997	Mass market brand Sonata launched.
February 1998	Karatmeter unveiled in Tanishq stores.
31 March 2002	Xerxes Desai retires from Titan.
1 April 2002	Bhaskar Bhat takes over as Titan's second managing director.
May 2002	Titan Edge launched.
April 2003	Tanishq's Golden Harvest scheme launched.
June 2004	Precision Engineering Division launched.
July 2004	Actor Aamir Khan signed on to endorse Titan.
September 2006	Titan Raga collection relaunched.
February 2007	Tanishq partners with the movie *Jodhaa Akbar* to make the jewellery used in the movie.
March 2007	Eyewear launched under Titan Eyeplus brand.
February 2009	The first Fastrack store launched on FC Road, Pune.
September 2013	Titan Skinn launched.
April 2013	Titan.co.in, Titan's e-commerce venture, launched.

December 2015	Titan's 1,000th store opens in Indira Nagar, Bengaluru.
January 2016	Titan Juxt, its first hybrid smart watch launched in collaboration with Hewlett-Packard.
27 June 2016	Titan founder Xerxes Desai passes away at the age of 79.
February 2017	Titan launches Taneira sarees, its newest brand.
November 2017	Titan Company Ltd crosses the $10 billion market capitalization milestone (approx. ₹64,000 crore).

FOREWORD

Titan is a company created by its people, their passion, dedication and belief. As the company celebrates 30 years of manufacturing and marketing excellence, Vinay Kamath's book is a timely look back at the strength and determination that was needed to ensure that Titan not only survived but also became a market leader by ruling the hearts of the Indian consumer, and in the process establishing itself as a jewel in the Tata crown.

Vinay's insights and ability to capture what lies at the heart of the company and the brand Titan – its people, or as they fondly call themselves, Titanians – is what will make this book so rewarding for readers. The protagonist of the Titan story is Xerxes Desai. Giving a befitting tribute to his contribution in building Titan and bringing out the power of an extraordinary team, Vinay's book provides glimpses into the roles played by these leaders in the Titan story in taking the company to where it is today.

Starting with watches in 1987 with Brand Titan, the company successfully launched into jewellery with Tanishq in 1995. It has since expanded into other lifestyle categories like eyewear

(Titan Eyeplus), accessories and fragrance (Skinn), and its latest, handcrafted sarees by Taneira, growing the company's revenues over five times and market capitalization over 17 times in the last decade, thus emerging as the third largest wealth creator for the Tata Group after Tata Motors and Tata Consultancy Services.

In line with the vision of our founder, Jamsetji Tata, Titanians not only focus on profits but also believe in contributing to society. Titan works towards the upliftment of the underprivileged girl child, skill development for the underprivileged, and the preservation and promotion of Indian arts, crafts and heritage.

With over 15 lifestyle and aspirational brands, a pan-India reach and the presence of 11,000 consumer touchpoints, state-of-the-art integrated manufacturing, cutting-edge in-house design and innovation, exceptional customer-orientation and service, and an undying spirit to conquer uncharted territories, I believe this people's company is marching to cater to aspirational India.

This foreword will be incomplete without a note of thanks to the Tamil Nadu Industrial Development Corporation (TIDCO) for believing in the Tata Group, leading to the birth of Titan back in 1984. I wish Bhaskar and his exceptional team the very best of luck in the coming years, and my compliments to Vinay for bringing this unique Tata story to life.

N. Chandrasekaran
Chairman, Tata Sons

PREFACE

The idea to write a book on Titan hit me while I was in the shower. I was rushing to meet with Titan Company Ltd's managing director, Bhaskar Bhat, after a company board meeting he had in Chennai. When I proposed the idea to him, Bhaskar was both receptive and cooperative. He gave me access to company insiders and helped set up key meetings and interviews. That's how this book got going over three years ago.

As a young reporter-cum-sub-editor with the *Times of India* in Bangalore in 1987, the year Titan launched its watches, I recall the buzz the brand had created. That was when Indian consumers were exposed to smart-looking watches at reasonable prices and the new quartz technology added to the excitement. In my interactions with several executives at Titan then, I was intrigued by the palpable excitement the young company generated.

Later, as a correspondent for *Business World* in Madras (now Chennai), I met the first Titan chairman, the late A.L. Mudaliar, at a party he had hosted at the Adyar Gate Hotel (it has since changed hands; it is the Crowne Plaza now) for Tamil Nadu's bureaucrats and notable citizens to celebrate the quick success of the company's watch project. It was he who introduced me to Titan's founding managing director, the charismatic Xerxes Desai, who then invited me to Hosur to visit Titan's plant and meet with its top management. Back in 1989, there were just two business magazines, one of which was *BusinessWorld*. The cover of its December issue mentioned an article titled 'The Triumph of Titan Watches'. Inside, it ran a five-page piece on Titan. I followed this up with a cover article in *BusinessWorld* featuring Xerxes, titled 'New Times at Titan'. Over the years, I have followed the company's progress and written about its various initiatives, and thus feel uniquely qualified to write a book about Titan as it completes 30 years as a brand remarkable for its innovative products and sparkling advertising.

Though it was launched in 1987, it could still be called a true child of liberalization with India opening up its markets in 1991. Titan was seen as a maverick brand that defied norms and brought freshness to the Indian consumer-goods market. Titan watches, Maruti cars and Hero Honda motorbikes became symbols of a new India that fired people's imagination. In this scenario, Titan was seen as trying to bring the best of the world into India, giving them a range of choices. A whole generation has grown up buying Titan watches to mark momentous occasions and has perhaps also transitioned to buying Fastrack bags, Tanishq jewellery, Titan eyewear and Skinn perfumes for themselves or as gifts.

Xerxes was always fond of saying that Titan was founded by sheer serendipity. 'Titan is often cited as a remarkable example of corporate success, featuring in management school case studies, but few know that we stumbled upon the opportunity to make watches almost accidentally and that it was a rather long and arduous but serendipitous journey,' he said. My long sessions with Xerxes at his gracious home in Bengaluru are perhaps the last conversations he had about the founding of Titan and its journey, before he passed away in June 2016.

As of 31 March 2018, cumulative production of Titan watches since its launch in April 1987 is a whopping 225 million, making it the fifth-largest integrated watchmaker in the world! Tanishq has emerged as perhaps the only national jewellery retail chain and Fastrack as an iconic youth brand. This is not to say it was all unalloyed success for Titan, despite all the awards and accolades that came its way. Nor was the enormous appeal it enjoyed almost immediately after its launch in the Indian market replicated in its other ventures. Indeed, its reputation as an ace marketer was badly punctured after its unsuccessful foray into Europe, which left the company deep in debt. Even Tanishq, today an enormously profitable brand, went through a decade of struggle before sales took off. The story of how Titan bounced back from its misadventures and went on to great triumph is told in this book.

Everyone, of course, knows Titan as a Tata company, but many will be surprised to know that Titan is actually a joint venture between the Tata Group and the Tamil Nadu government. During the pre-liberalization era, the Tamil Nadu Industrial Development Corporation (TIDCO) was one of the few organizations with a licence to manufacture watches. Partnering with TIDCO enabled the creation of Titan. Now, over 30 years later, Titan Company Ltd, in which both own almost equal stakes, could well be called a jewel in the crown for the Tamil Nadu government with Titan's market capitalization soaring; Titan has paid over ₹450 crore in cumulative dividends to TIDCO over the years. Three past chairmen of the company, all Indian Administrative Service (IAS) officers and Tamil Nadu government bureaucrats, and the present chairman, K. Gnanadesikan, have expressed their happiness with the Tata management and the enormous success Titan has enjoyed. Today, Titan stands out as a shining example of a business model in the joint sector of the state government. TIDCO has been content to let the Tatas run the company while the chairmanship is always with a TIDCO nominee.

I have bought many Titan watches over the years, to wear and to gift; the most recent one was a present for my daughter to mark the beginning of her life as a college student. For our twentieth wedding anniversary, I secretly bought Tanishq jewellery for my wife – she was pleasantly surprised, not least because, as she said, she didn't know I knew how to buy jewellery! I wear glasses purchased at Titan Eyeplus and sometimes spray myself with Skinn perfume. Perhaps the next present I give my wife will be a Taneira saree! I am sure thousands of households around the country are similarly touched by Titan's products.

This book is the result of scores of conversations with Titanians, past and present. Even those who have moved on to other jobs and positions share a special bond with the company, and they too have shared their experiences. It tells the story of how the company was built, through the voices of the numerous talented and dynamic people who have made Titan what it is: one of the best-known homegrown brands in India and quite clearly a tremendously successful consumer business.

ONE

LUCK BY CHANCE

It was a hot and humid day in May 1975, and Xerxes Desai was irked with himself. He had just visited Naval Mody, the head of Tata Inc., New York, then on a visit to Bombay (now Mumbai), only to discover that he had called on the wrong Mody. Xerxes needed to speak to Minoo Mody, who had recently taken over as the first chief executive officer of Tata Sons, the Group's holding company for its multifarious businesses.

Minoo, much younger than the other directors on the board of Tata Sons at the time, had moved to the Tata Group from the audit firm, A.F. Ferguson. Bright, resolute and flamboyant, he would come to play a decisive role in Xerxes's future, a fact unbeknownst to the dapper Parsi as he placed a call to Bombay House, the headquarters of the Tata Group, for an appointment with the right Mody. Neither of them could have imagined that the call would set in motion a chain of events that would bring together a group of remarkable people who would create Titan Watches (later Titan Company Ltd, revenues of ₹15,656 crore in the financial year 2017–2018 with a net profit of ₹1,163 crore).

Back then in the mid-1970s, 38-year-old Xerxes was just coming to the end of an assignment with the City and Industrial Development Corporation of Maharashtra (CIDCO) to whom he had been on loan from the Tatas for his project management expertise. The project was the development of New Bombay (now Navi Mumbai), a massive town planned by the government of Maharashtra on the mainland across from the seven islands of the old city. The promoters of CIDCO had put together a remarkable team of town planners, architects, transport planners, economists, educationists, sociologists and operations research specialists, apart from civil, mechanical and electrical engineers for the purpose. It was this eclectic mix of people that Xerxes had been working with.

A graduate of New College, Oxford, where he read philosophy, politics and economics, Xerxes had joined the Tata Administrative Service (TAS) in 1961 and worked for several years with the Taj Group, rebuilding and renovating the iconic Taj Mahal Palace hotel in Bombay and constructing the InterContinental next door. Later, he was appointed project manager for the picturesque Fort Aguada Resort in Goa, the Taj Coromandel in Madras (now Chennai) and the Lake Palace hotel in Udaipur.

'I was done building hotels for the rich,' recalled Xerxes in his measured drawl, over the course of several conversations on how Titan Company Ltd came to be, at his graciously appointed bungalow in the leafy enclave of Indira Nagar in Bengaluru in 2016, a shade over 40 years since his first phone call to Minoo Mody. Recalling the old days, he said that when the CIDCO opportunity arose, J.R.D. Tata (J.R.D.), Chairman, Tata Sons, and its directors, Jamshed Bhabha, who administered TAS, and Nani Palkhivala, the eminent lawyer whose opinion J.R.D. sought on most issues, reluctantly agreed to a secondment. In other words, they were agreeable to Xerxes being deputed to CIDCO for a short period of time. 'But since CIDCO could afford to pay only about a third of the salary that I was drawing in Indian Hotels – a staggering ₹3,500 per month! – it was agreed that the Tatas would bear one-third, I would take a cut of one-third and CIDCO would pay the balance one-third. It was financially ruinous but hugely beneficial in other ways,' said Xerxes. Xerxes spent two and a half years at CIDCO, where he worked with legends such as architect Charles Correa, urban planner Shirish Patel and managing director J.B. D'Souza, an IAS officer highly respected as an administrator. There was also Anil Manchanda, an operations research specialist and industrial engineer, ten years his junior. With a Master's degree in statistics from the Indian Statistical Institute (ISI), Calcutta (now Kolkata), Anil was in the operations research and systems task force and was executive assistant to Shirish Patel who was the technical advisor on the project. Although Xerxes and Anil didn't know it then, over the next 25 years their lives would be inextricably entwined.

Xerxes's first task at CIDCO had been as project manager for the Vashi township, the first phase of the New Bombay project. After a year or so, he was tasked with taking on the role of general manager for the whole project, which included functions covering planning, design and construction. However, towards the end of his third year with CIDCO, he was under pressure to return to the Tata fold while CIDCO wanted him to quit the Tatas and become a full-time public servant.

'Quite naturally, the Tatas offered a working environment that no other organization in India could equal,' said Xerxes. 'And there was also the sobering fact that after working for 13 years, I had no savings whatsoever; in fact, I was in debt!' The question then arose about Xerxes's next posting in the Tata Group. Indian Hotels, which owns the Taj Group and where he had worked earlier, didn't have a vacancy for him at the time. The National Radio & Electronics Company (NELCO), then run directly by Ratan Tata, the future chairman of the Tata Group, had an opening but a brief meeting between Xerxes and Ratan didn't yield much. Jamshed Bhabha and Minoo Mody were the chairman and vice chairman respectively of Tata Press, a wholly owned Tata company, and at that juncture headless and loss-making. They secured the approval of J.R.D. and Nani Palkhivala to task Xerxes with turning around the ailing Tata Press, one of Minoo's direct charges.

At the time, Tata Press was an obscure and poorly performing company, printing art and culture magazines, calendars and diaries, annual reports, computer stationery and books. The assignment did not appeal to Xerxes. However, he had not reckoned with Minoo whose financially savvy chartered accountant's mind had always chafed over the fact that Tata Press was wholly Tata-owned while other Tata Group companies leveraged public funds through the equity market to grow. He laid the bait for Xerxes, spelling out a vision of taking Tata Press public and using the money thus raised to do something that was bigger and hopefully more interesting. Xerxes was immediately taken with the challenge. Besides, what choice did he have? So he told Minoo, 'If I am to be strong-armed into joining this company, I'll join it if it can be used as a springboard to venture into new areas.'

When Xerxes discussed his situation with Anil, by then a friend from their CIDCO days, and confessed to his apprehensions regarding turning around Tata Press, the irrepressible Anil assured him that although it called for detailed work, method studies and efficient management of operations, it wouldn't be difficult. Before joining CIDCO, Anil had been in industrial consulting and had been trained in work study, method study and efficiency management. 'Would you like to join Tata Press, then, along with me?' Xerxes asked Anil. It was tempting. The New Bombay project had started off well, the master plan had been presented to the government, and CIDCO had already built the first phase of around 1,000 houses in Vashi. The next phase would involve expanding it, and that would mean more of the same. By then, Anil was also wary of the bureaucracy beginning to take hold of CIDCO. 'Let's give five years to turn [Tata Press] around and also start a new project,' he told Xerxes.

It took just one meeting for Minoo to warm to Anil. Xerxes joined Tata Press in mid-1975 as general manager; Anil followed a few months later as systems manager. 'Minoo and I got along well, but he was not sure of what Xerxes and I could do. He told me as much. "Xerxes seems to think you guys will make a good team to take it on, so go ahead," he told me,' Anil recalls, while speaking about the three years it took to overhaul the company, both in terms of personnel and machinery.

It began with Xerxes identifying another Anil who would also make a significant contribution to Tata Press. This was Anil Gore, a graduate of Cambridge University and Xerxes's neighbour in Colaba, Bombay. Having worked initially at the ad agency, Lintas, Gore was later director of marketing at the pressure cooker makers Hawkins. He had quit Hawkins following differences with the management and was contemplating what to do. That's when Xerxes walked into Anil Manchanda's office and asked whether they could use someone like Gore as the old-guard managers were leaving Tata Press, unable to cope with the change and productivity demanded of them. 'At that time,' says Anil, 'I was heading multiple departments, including sales and marketing. Xerxes didn't say so but Gore's induction involved bringing in someone who'd outrank me. [However] I didn't hesitate, knowing that this would only be temporary and that I would catch up.' Gore joined Tata Press as general manager, marketing, in 1977. With Gore taking charge of marketing and sales, Xerxes and Anil, now as general manager, development, were able to concentrate on bringing about some pretty drastic changes in terms of equipment, work processes, human resources management, marketing and salesmanship, smart bidding for jobs, better financial controls and, of course, sound business management practices. In the process, they also cleaned up some minor corruption in the purchase and sales departments. They built a solid management team, which included a strong production chief and finance head.

With Tata Press well on the way to recovery, the trio of Minoo, Xerxes and Anil began scouring for interesting projects to diversify into. Xerxes and Anil rejected many ideas that came from Minoo; he, however, took this in the right spirit because he always got a detailed note on why a particular idea wouldn't work. Among the projects suggested were the manufacture of shipping containers, gelatin and carbon black.

At the time, no one could have imagined that a little-known company of the Tata Group would be the launch pad for Titan Watches, now among India's best-known consumer brands. But, business decisions, as Xerxes always held, though seemingly the result of meticulous planning, often happen by chance.

It was at this juncture, in the late 1970s, that the extraordinary bureaucrat-scholar Iravatham Mahadevan came into the picture. At that time, Mahadevan, an IAS officer of the Tamil Nadu cadre, was a joint secretary in the Ministry of Industrial Development in New Delhi. That apart, he was a Jawaharlal Nehru scholar on leave from the IAS, studying the Indus Script and using the computing facilities and expertise at the Tata Institute of Fundamental Research (TIFR) in Mumbai to analyse the complete collection of discovered texts with a view towards printing and publishing it as a concordance (a comprehensive appearance-based alphabetical list). The computerized analysis was nearing completion and Mahadevan was at his wit's end trying to locate a printer who could handle an unknown and unreadable script. One day, Dr Mathai Joseph who headed the computer science facility at TIFR and was a friend of Xerxes's wife Rajani, called Xerxes and asked if Tata Press would like to take a look at it.

'Sure, tell him to come and talk to Anil and me,' Xerxes replied. Anil had been working with mainframe computers since 1964 while still a student at the ISI and had also worked with the TIFR team while at CIDCO. Tata Press was at this time also printing the Bombay telephone directory from magnetic tapes created by Tata Consultancy Services (TCS). It was quickly established that TIFR could generate the Indus Script texts on magnetic tapes coded to suit Tata Press requirements. The problem was that there were no fonts to print the script. While the Alphatype equipment used by Tata Press was the finest available, it wasn't smart enough to tell the Indus Script apart from the English language for which it was designed. Anil assigned the task of finding a solution to K.P. Rao, a self-taught electronics tinkerer who, working with the studio and art departments of Tata Press, was able to develop the appropriate fonts. They then produced photo positives directly from the computer tapes, ready for printing on offset machines.

'That was a breakthrough of sorts because no one else had figured it out till then,' recalls Anil during a long conversation in the old-worldly environs of the Bangalore Club in Bengaluru. 'I spent many late nights at TIFR after my regular work to ensure that what they produced would talk to our machines. The fact that TIFR's food supplier, Air India's hotel subsidiary Hotel Corporation of India, served five-star stuff at Udupi-restaurant prices was a great help. In good time we were ready to print and did some test runs. Our people had, of course, no idea how to proofread it. That monumental burden eventually fell entirely on Mahadevan.'

While the process was under way there wasn't much for Mahadevan to do, so he resumed work in Delhi. The printing project took over six months, during which time Mahadevan was a frequent visitor to Tata Press. One day, over a lunch of sandwiches and tea, Xerxes and Anil mentioned to Mahadevan their hitherto unsuccessful search for a new project. 'Look, why doesn't Anil come up to Delhi and we will help you identify some projects that the Tatas could consider,' said Mahadevan.

The offer was accepted almost before he had completed his sentence, and as soon as Mahadevan went back, Anil set off for New Delhi. For three days he parked himself on a sofa in Mahadevan's cavernous office in Udyog Bhavan while a steady stream of visitors went in and out of the room. The drearily furnished office was enlivened by endless cups of excellent coffee from the canteen run by India Coffee House and the gossip and chatter of bureaucrats at work. 'In between Mahadevan's other tasks,' Anil recalls, 'we discussed various projects. I showed interest in four or five areas, and Mahadevan called [in] his people from various departments with their files and I pored over the data, which were basically industry snapshots.' There were reports for all kinds of projects, from ophthalmic glass to granite tombstones to mechanized fishing boats. And then there were watches. According to an introductory note penned by Xerxes for the Titan staff newsletter, on the fourth day, 21 March 1977, at about 10 p.m., Anil phoned Xerxes and laid out the options. 'There are five projects I've shortlisted. The best among them is watches,' he said.

From all accounts, it seems that in the 1970s, Indians wanted watches that the rest of the world was wearing. Swiss brands such as Favre Leuba (which Titan bought in late 2011 for €2 million, which was equivalent to ₹13.8 crore at the time), Roamer, Sandoz, Titoni and West End, and Japanese brands such as Seiko and Citizen, were being smuggled into the country. And that's what consumers wanted: smart-looking, foreign, branded watches. These were available in abundance at watch stores in the big cities; more so in places like the Fort area in Mumbai and Connaught Place in New Delhi, recalls Anil. One could even request a specific brand and model and get it on the spot or delivered soon enough. These watches were provided a full warranty by the retailer, normally for one year, but often for longer. Typically, the shops that sold these watches were family businesses that many of the international watch companies had dealt with for years, mentions Anil.

Upon his return to Bombay, Anil, Xerxes and Gore had their first meeting to discuss fresh plans. Excitement ran high among the three. 'We could see that there was definitely a large market and local makers were unable to meet the demand. The fact that we did not know anything about watches didn't daunt us. We knew we could hire the technical talent,' says Anil.

The team did two things after this meeting: the first was to commission a study by Tata Economic Consultancy Services (TECS) and the second was to prepare an internal note for Minoo Mody on the proposal for a watch-manufacturing company. Minoo in turn made a strong case for watches to J.R.D. that got him just as excited. After all, the picture looked good: high-precision engineering, state-of-the-art electronics, the potential to enter the high fashion segment and a projected consumer base of one billion Indians by the end of the century.

Within a few weeks of Anil's visit to Mahadevan in New Delhi, Xerxes and Anil had a couple of briefing sessions with Minoo, in the course of which they reviewed the TECS research with him. One morning soon after, Xerxes received a hand-written note from Minoo on a small, monogrammed sheet of paper which read: 'Please send a detailed note on The Watch Project for Jeh.' Senior directors were encouraged to address J.R.D. Tata as Jeh as he was known within his family (short for Jehangir, his first name). And 'The Watch Project' it remained till the founding of the company many years later.

At the time, the only significant Indian watchmaker was HMT. It made excellent watches but, as old-timers jocularly recall, HMT seemed to be not so much in the watch *marketing* business as in the watch *rationing* business, as demand greatly outstripped supply. At times, there would be a waiting list for a particular model. All told, in the 1970s, HMT and a few small-scale manufacturers produced just about one and a half million watches annually for the entire Indian market – HMT made around one million and the smaller players another half a million. Allwyn, a venture of the Andhra Pradesh government set up in 1981, was also a key player although not in the league of HMT. In any case, according to Anil, Allwyn's annual numbers did not cross one million, although its plastic-cased sporty quartz range called Allwyn Trendy became very popular. Even so, there was a comfortable space for smuggled watches, showing that demand was nowhere near being met. The very first estimates of market size came from research by TECS. Their figures were based on government data pertaining to local manufacturers and derived from customs seizures. (Gold and watches were the two most frequently smuggled and valuable contraband items seized at the time.)

Utilizing Gore's familiarity with the advertising and publications businesses, the Tata Press team connected with the National Readership Survey (NRS) which was commissioned by a consortium of newspaper and magazine publishers to assess readership of various publications. The NRS was a very large format national survey conducted by the Indian Market Research Bureau (IMRB) and a few other research outfits. To help defray the expenses, the organizers of the survey accepted a few questions from advertisers and potential advertisers that they would 'tag on'. Tata Press paid for asking supplementary questions which were appended to the main questionnaire. These questions pertained to watch ownership, watch and owner age, owner sex, purchase occasion and location of purchase. '[The results from the survey] allowed us to get fairly good estimates of watch ownership and we estimated purchase patterns based on a 10-year ownership cycle, including hand-me-downs as people progressed in life via a job or marriage, a promotion or graduation,' explains Anil.

Apart from the watches supplied by local manufacturers, a large number were smuggled into the country and sold and serviced through a well-oiled retail network. Anil refers to this quite unequivocally when he says, 'The smuggling process was fairly well organized and had been fairly well written about in the press at that time, as also in fiction and film.' Retailers sold these products only in certain markets and, naturally, could not provide a formal receipt or bill, but instead offered an informal warranty which the Swiss and Japanese watchmakers ensured was honoured. Regulations in the 1970s were stringent as foreign exchange was scarce. The import of watches was totally banned; even a single watch brought in by a traveller invited a stiff penalty. All bags would be searched for items like jewellery, watches and cameras.

When the Xerxes-Anil duo plumped for watches as their next line of business, Mahadevan, who happened to be the chairman of a task force on the watch manufacturing industry, supported the choice. However, there was a small problem: the manufacture of watches was reserved for the small-scale sector. While government-owned large public-sector units were also allowed to make watches, large private-sector groups such as the Tatas were not allowed to enter watch manufacture under the existing rules. Anil clarifies that the socialist economic policies of the government of the day sought to control the means of production and generate employment. Therefore, in such a climate, it was the public sector and small-scale entrepreneurs who were given a boost. Mahadevan, however, did not concur with this policy and felt that the Tatas could try to have it overturned.

While all this was going on, the work of turning Tata Press around was proceeding apace. It was now the most modern press in India. But judging from international trade magazines on the printing industry, it trailed the rest of the world in many ways. To create a road map to modernization, it was decided that Anil would visit the largest international technology and trade fair for the printing industry in Dusseldorf, Germany.

Interestingly, even though 'watches' were not in the field of vision of the Tata Group companies in the mid-1970s, the Tatas had been associated with Swiss watchmaker Favre Leuba, a brand very popular in India. He remembers seeing a huge Favre Leuba billboard in Chowringhee, Calcutta. 'I persuaded an uncle of mine to gift me that particular watch!' says Anil. When Minoo mentioned The Watch Project over lunch at Bombay House, one of the senior directors recalled the past connection and suggested that Anil could reignite these talks since he was headed to Europe. There were no files or papers to throw light on what exactly had happened. So a fresh approach was made and thus, 1977 came to be a watershed year: a turning point for Tata Press and a start for Titan.

In June that year, Anil took off for Germany with $1,024 (₹8,700) in forex for a three-week trip. Funnily enough, his original forex application to the Reserve Bank of India (RBI) was rejected. Anil confirms that it was eventually sanctioned only because Xerxes knew R.K. Hazari, the then deputy governor of the RBI, who had earlier worked with the *Economic & Political Weekly* where Rajani, Xerxes's wife, also worked. No explanations were offered for the rejection of an application. In Anil's case, for instance, despite Hazari's intervention, the RBI cut down the number of his days of travel as well as the daily allowance.

After a mind-blowing exposure to modern printing technology at the trade fair, Anil went on to Bienne, the heart of the Swiss watch industry. His guide was Ernst Mayor, then in his 70s and the last chief executive of Favre Leuba, which had folded up in the mid-1970s. Like many other Swiss brands, it could not counter the cheaper Japanese watches or quickly move to quartz technology. Mayor had arranged a three-day programme for Anil which included visits to several watch units. At that stage, with no governmental approvals in place, Tata Press could not progress beyond the dream of making watches, but, as Anil says, 'This visit really opened my eyes to what the watch industry involved in terms of technology, skill, training and investments.'

While Tata Press pursued licensing opportunities, Minoo's job was to get the senior Tata directors and chiefs of other group companies on board. They would be asked to invest in the new company's capital along with Tata Press. In the 1970s and 1980s, the various large companies of the Tata Group were run by influential individuals with the capacity to invest, such as Ajit Kerkar (chairman and managing director, Indian Hotels Company), Russi Mody (chairman, Tata Iron and Steel Company Ltd [TISCO], now Tata Steel), Sumant Moolgaokar (managing director, Tata Engineering and Locomotive Company [TELCO], now Tata Motors), Darbari Seth (managing director, Tata Chemicals) and Naval Tata (chairman, Tata Electric). Minoo knew it wouldn't be easy to sell them the idea that the watch-making industry would make for a good investment and that the Tata Press team was the right one to execute the project.

'I faced a lot of opposition from within the Tata Group while starting Titan. Indeed, one senior director, Mr Palkhivala, called me in and actually begged me to give up the project. He said that directors like me should not pursue or manage projects but focus on fortifying the reputation of the Tatas. My principal task at that time was to protect Xerxes and his team from being demotivated. I insulated them from this hostile atmosphere and did not let them know the state of affairs at Tata Sons' board level. The majority of the senior directors were opposed to getting into the watch business. And the only reason why I was able to push through the project was [because of] the support of J.R.D. Tata,'

Minoo, now in his mid-80s, explains during a conversation over coffee on the veranda of the upscale Willingdon Club in South Mumbai. 'Nobody, especially J.R.D., ever looked at the numbers. The decision was based on the premise that if you trusted Minoo you would approve his proposal,' he adds.

Many of the old Tata hands felt the technology was too sophisticated to absorb. 'The previous experience the Tatas had with sophisticated technology [Tata Precision, Singapore] also weighed heavily on their minds,' said Minoo. Tata Precision had been set up to make moulds for injection-moulding machines for plastic components. It had an initial order from Siemens but the product was rejected and the business had ceased. 'We could not achieve the precision required by them. Subsequently, [we] got orders for moulds requiring less precision, but the business just about broke even. Mr Moolgaokar, who was in charge of Tata Precision, was convinced that the degree of sophistication required for watch movements was beyond our capacity and, for that reason, did not support the project,' recalls Minoo.

The fact that J.R.D. backed a project which was way outside the Tata comfort zone, being developed by an Oxford humanities graduate and an Indian Statistical Institute postgraduate with no precision industry experience between them, was a huge morale booster. As Xerxes wrote in the very first issue of *Watchword,* the Titan newsletter, in March 1988: 'There had been times in the intervening years when we felt weary of the effort needed to find a partner, negotiate a know-how contract and get governmental approvals in the teeth of opposition by smugglers and entrenched Indian manufacturers. There were times when Minoo, Anil and I felt like abandoning the effort. But, there was one man who thought that the effort should not slacken. That was J.R.D. Tata!'

Eventually, only four Tata companies would contribute to Titan's equity, each of them because of the support of the directors of the companies – Tata Sons (J.R.D.), Tata Steel (Russi Mody), Tata Chemicals (Darbari Seth) and Tata Electric (thanks to Kersi Gherda, the managing director, in spite of Naval Tata, the chairman, being opposed to the proposal). Minoo brought in the cash-rich associate company, *Reader's Digest* India, to make up the balance. *Reader's Digest* was then owned by a few directors of the Tata Group in their individual capacity and by some other prominent persons and artists; they had bought the American company as the Janata government in the late 1970s did not want any foreign capital presence in Indian media.

Apart from garnering support from the chiefs of major Tata companies, it was also important to have on their side Ratan Tata, who was heading Tata Industries. Anil recalls that Minoo assigned this task to him and Xerxes. Armed with the same note that had gone to J.R.D., the two had a brief meeting with Ratan who was not entirely convinced. Until then, the Tata Group's experience in consumer-facing businesses hadn't been happy. None of NELCO's ventures had succeeded; it was financially supported by Tata Electric throughout its existence, recalls Minoo. Another consumer-facing business that struggled was Tata Oil Mills (TOMCO), eventually sold to its major competitor, Hindustan Unilever. Tata companies did well in heavy manufacturing with companies such as Tata Steel (TISCO then) and Tata Motors (erstwhile TELCO). Later, Ratan, as the Tata Group's chairman, would show support for the company and visit the Titan factory in Hosur in April 1992. Clearly it was Titan's success that won him over.

The team's first task was to get a technical collaborator for the most crucial part of a watch, the movement, which drives the hands. At that time, there were just five large and integrated watchmakers who could have supplied the technical know-how: Citizen, Seiko, Timex, Casio and ASUAG (now SMH, the Swiss company that makes Swatch). But Citizen had already tied up with HMT, Seiko was in the process of tying up with Allwyn, Timex was in financial trouble, and Casio had only just started making watches and was concentrating on digital. This left the Swiss, who had categorically declared they would not part with their watch-making technology.

Around this time, in the mid-1970s, digital watches had emerged out of nowhere with a bang and started making a big splash in the international marketplace, threatening the balance of the industry. Almost all major mechanical watchmakers were jolted out of their complacence. Suddenly, for under $5 or ₹137, a consumer could get a wristwatch that outperformed the most complex mechanical watches, even a Rolex, in accuracy. Every watchmaker, big and small, was starting to make digital watches, as were many companies that originally manufactured electronic components and products.

Xerxes and Anil felt this new digital technology needed to be explored. Through Tata Precision in Singapore, they established contact with Fairchild Semiconductors, makers of integrated circuits and transistors, which also had a liquid crystal display (LCD) and digital watch business. Xerxes took off for California where Fairchild was headquartered. The company had an assembly line in Hong Kong which they wanted to sell. The deal was for the Tatas to buy the line and keep using Fairchild chips and LCDs for digital watches. But the Indian government quickly poured cold water on this plan. The Electronics Commission, then led by the physicist and policymaker M.G.K. Menon, mandated that the Tatas should source LCD technology from the National Physical Laboratory (NPL) in Delhi. The government wanted Fairchild to provide chip-making technology via the Tatas to a public sector company, and demanded that the chips be 'Made in India'. But this made little sense in the context as NPL had nothing in the works except a few leaky, slow-response and poor-contrast displays sourced from the erstwhile USSR. Plus, there was no way a plant for the fabrication of chips could be justified on the basis of the requirements of one start-up watchmaker, recalls Anil.

The government's approach ended up helping the Tatas avoid an expensive misstep, because the popularity of digital watches started slipping just as quickly as it had risen, and they rapidly became low-priced novelty gift items. Anil recalls the postmortems of this phenomenon in watch-industry journals which concluded that the decline had come about for two basic reasons: the limited styling options and the time required to register analogue time being just a small fraction of the time needed to check time on a digital watch. Anil explains that the human eye perceives and registers analogue images faster than it does digital data. 'No one needs to know that it is 06:13:29 but for most purposes it's a quarter past six. It takes perceptibly longer to register the former.' Digital watches fast fell out of favour. Very quickly, big brands such as Citizen and Seiko started making analogue electronic watches with the same accuracy levels as the digital ones. Initially expensive, the costs dropped fast and within a few years analogue watch movements became cheaper than mechanical movements.

During this transition period, Tata Press's ambitions to be a watchmaker remained in the doldrums. Tata Press made an unsuccessful attempt to buy Hegde and Golay (H&G), a Bangalore-based quartz watchmaker. The acquisition plan was aborted when it became clear that the H&G operation was unviable due to technical, manufacturing and financial reasons. Meanwhile, a lot of money had been spent on The Watch Project and Minoo's primary job remained protecting the team and ensuring that no one questioned the lack of progress in their initiatives.

But fortune came to the rescue once again in the shape of Iravatham Mahadevan who, in September 1979, was posted as chairman and managing director of Tamil Nadu Industrial Development Corporation (TIDCO). As Xerxes recounted,

'One day he [Mahadevan] called me from Madras. He had just discovered that TIDCO had been in dialogue with a French movement manufacturer, France Ebauches, but was yet to find a joint-venture partner to execute [its watch-making] project, and would Tata Press be interested. And, of course, we were!'

Xerxes and Anil went to Madras to meet with Mahadevan, who said he was glad that Tata Press was still interested in making watches. Before he took over as managing director of TIDCO, the industry promotion body had sounded out a few local industrial houses to partner with them, with no success. At the meeting, Mahadevan called in the project manager in charge of watches, told him of the Tata interest and requested him to brief Xerxes and Anil and to hand over the project files for them to study. Over two days – in swimming trunks, reclining on beach loungers at the Fisherman's Cove, a Taj luxury property 50 km from the city – Xerxes and Anil pored over the project papers. At the end of the second day, their decision was unanimous: 'Yes, let's do it!'

Now in his 80s, Mahadevan, who resides in a suburb of Chennai, is self-effacing about his role in the project. 'I encouraged the project on merit and didn't tie it [up] in red tape,' he says. 'While I did my best to get Titan off the ground, it was my successors who as MDs of TIDCO took the project forward.'

T.K. Arun, who retired as general manager and secretary of TIDCO and was a member of Titan's board for several years, was a junior executive with the company in the early 1980s working on development projects. 'Our job was to identify an opportunity and take it to a particular level, secure the clearances and then pick a capable investor to take the project forward,' explains Arun as we speak at the TIDCO headquarters in Chennai. Their mandate was to create manufacturing jobs in order to bolster employment. A watch project fitted the bill perfectly and this one, says Arun, 'had a real multiplier effect in creating jobs.'

With the Tatas coming in as TIDCO's joint-venture partner, things moved swiftly. The central government had issued licences for watch-making to a few state governments. TIDCO, as a government agency, could get a letter of intent to make watches but needed an industry partner to spearhead the project in what it called the joint sector. Once it had the Tata buy-in, it reactivated contact with the French. Soon, Xerxes and Anil, accompanied by a TIDCO project engineer, were on a flight out to Besançon in France to get acquainted with France Ebauches and take the project forward. However, the president of France Ebauches, François Perret, was unable to meet them as he had sprained his ankle playing tennis and sent word that if they wished they could meet the marketing chief. 'We swallowed our pride and met with this gentleman who took us around their plants and explained what they could do,' said Xerxes. 'Fortune seemed to be favouring us once again. Negotiations, though protracted, went reasonably well and we painstakingly cobbled together a technical collaboration agreement over something like a two-year period.'

Perret and his team visited India to seal the deal. J.R.D. was requested to be present at Bombay House to sign off on it. The son of a French mother, J.R.D. spoke French fluently and Minoo needed him for the final negotiations because even though Perret knew English well, at the meetings he spoke only in French. As it turns out, J.R.D. and Perret got along famously.

'It was very interesting; I would talk to Mr Tata in English and he would talk to Perret in French, and this is how we went through the key clauses and finally got to the fee, which was 45 million francs [₹5.8 crore]. Now, when we got to this point, for the first time Mr Tata spoke to me in Gujarati as he didn't want Team Perret to understand what we were saying. I was surprised and, in fact, till that point of time, didn't even know that Mr Tata could speak Gujarati. Later he told me that he learnt it from the servants in his house!' recalls Minoo chuckling.

J.R.D. asked Minoo in Gujarati, 'What should I do? Do I accept this figure?' Minoo told him to accept the offer but to demand more in return, such as training more technicians for a longer period of time. J.R.D. turned to Perret and did just that. Perret had been having a bad year financially and was keen on this deal. 'He was happy [with the terms] and we sealed the deal,' says Minoo.

The Tata Group, TIDCO and France Ebauches put their stamp on the alliance at a signing ceremony in June 1983 in Paris's prestigious Pavillon Gabriel in the gardens of the Champs-Élysées, a stone's throw from the Place de la Concorde. At the event J.R.D. Tata was invited to be the guest of honour, and the distinguished French statesman, Edgar Faure (who, coincidentally, had attended the same school in France as J.R.D.) was invited too. But their troubles hadn't ended. Even at the event everything that could go wrong, did, recalled Xerxes. The temperature in Paris was a torrid 38°C, and in the absence of fans and air-conditioning in that historic hall, without even windows for cross ventilation, everybody was melting in their suits. Minoo read out a short speech in English, but what followed was a French translation not of the speech that had just been delivered, but of a long and dreary draft sent earlier to France Ebauches for translation and rejected by J.R.D.! The flags in front of the signatories' stands sported the French colours red, white and blue, but in the wrong sequence. 'To cap it all, the French had forgotten to bring the contract to be signed, so we signed blank pieces of paper, hoping they were out of view of the audience and the cameras,' said Xerxes chuckling at the memory. Fortunately, Jacques Chirac, then mayor of Paris – and later to be President of France – who was expected to attend, didn't turn up. At the end of the day, however, the event ended on a backslapping note.

Now that the ink was on paper, they turned their attention to getting the operations going in India. Minoo, Xerxes and Anil went to New Delhi to seek backing from the Indian government to enter the watch-making business. But yet again they faced a roadblock. The Secretary of the Ministry of Commerce and Industry, Arun Ghosh, dismissed them peremptorily, saying that the Tatas would never be allowed to make watches as this sector was reserved for public and small-scale industries. His attitude left Minoo red in the face. Anil says of that meeting, 'Xerxes looked away in disbelief. I was the junior-most and quite amused that we had gone all the way to Delhi for just a quick brush-off.' Minoo recalls, 'I also had a private meeting with a senior minister who offered to give us a licence provided we set up the unit in his constituency. I flatly refused, insisting on our right to choose the place.'

And so it was back to square one, back to frustration. Months went by. By this time, Tata Press had had a public issue, made a lot of money and was in a good place. Were the stars indicating it was expedient to abandon the project?

The year 1984 brought with it seismic changes in India. Following the assassination of Prime Minister Indira Gandhi in October 1984, her son Rajiv Gandhi became prime minister. With the change in the country's leadership there came a turnaround in the approach to management of the Indian economy and the role the private sector and large businesses could play. The time appeared right for The Watch Project.

However, the Tatas preferred to be cautious and sought advice on the matter from a consultant retained by Tata Press. He was clear that while the government had not yet formally revised the policy on watch manufacturing, they were likely to look the other way if others entered the fray. In early 1985 he advised them to put in a fresh application for a joint venture between TIDCO and a little-known private company whose provenance would be known only to senior bureaucrats. The Tata name was not to figure in this application. The fear was that some junior official, still sticking to the old ways, would hold up the file. 'So, we did just that. We put in an application in the name of Questar Investments with a handful of us, including Minoo, Anil and myself, as the promoters. After all, we had nothing to lose, so far it had been a star-crossed quest. However, as a salve to our conscience, and somewhat cussedly, we named the new company Titan Watches. Titan was an acronym for Tata Industries and Tamil Nadu: "T" and "I" for Tata Industries and "TAN" for Tamil Nadu. And so, finally and adventitiously, this long-gestated venture came to see the light of day,' elaborated Xerxes.

Questar, a private limited company, had no significant capital, and was truly small-scale when it signed the joint venture with TIDCO. After the joint-venture agreement was signed, TIDCO applied to the central government for final project approval, which it gave without asking any questions about the antecedents of Questar. Questar would later be taken over by the Tatas via a rights issue to which the original promoters would not subscribe, to formalize their involvement in the project. 'Fortunately, by this time, governmental prejudices had been partially shed and big business houses were no longer that unwelcome,' said Xerxes.

With this, the Tatas' ambition to manufacture watches took another step forward. Destiny beckoned. It was almost eight years since Anil had mentioned the word 'wristwatches' to Xerxes in a 10 p.m. phone call from Delhi. Until it had emerged from a welter of projects in Mahadevan's office, the word 'wristwatch' had not been on anyone's wishlist at the Tatas. Both Xerxes and Anil had not really wanted to work in a printing press, even though it was the biggest in India; Minoo Mody had used their ambition to suggest Tata Press as a base to establish a more interesting project and give themselves jobs to their liking.

Xerxes was fond of saying that Titan was founded by sheer serendipity. 'Titan is often cited as a remarkable example of corporate success, featuring in management school case studies;

but few know that we stumbled upon the opportunity to make watches almost accidentally and that it was a rather long and arduous but serendipitous journey,' he said.

'A bit more accurately,' says Anil, 'we stumbled onto it because we went looking for non-humdrum jobs for ourselves and Minoo, happily played guardian and guiding angel.' Minoo, skilfully, patiently and steadfastly shepherded the project through a long gestation period, keeping all naysayers at bay. Without Anil, it was unlikely that Tata Press would have taken up Mahadevan's technically complex, for its time, project to print his Indus Script concordance. Without Mahadevan's offer to explore projects along with him, any new Tata Press project would most likely have been something connected to printing. 'Without Xerxes there would have been no project. He made Titan what it is. He created a fairly unique culture which would serve Titan well for decades,' says Anil. And, without Maryanne D'Souza, the project secretary, who, as Anil's personal assistant, single-handedly managed the project documentation, communications and logistics for almost a decade until the team moved to Bengaluru, the process could have been far more strenuous than it was. Probably most remarkable was the fact that in short order a super-talented management team emerged virtually out of nowhere. By mid-1985, managerial recruitment and planning commenced. Manufacturing started in late 1986, and in March 1987, exactly a decade after the word 'watches' was first uttered by the team, Titan Watches was launched.

A sense of excitement and expectation pervaded the atmosphere as J.R.D. dedicated the manufacturing complex at Hosur, Tamil Nadu, to the country at a commemorative function on 11 March 1988, with a huge pan-national folk festival unlike any other, in a factory laid out as a garden. The Titan dedication ceremony was attended by a few thousand guests from all over India including most of the senior Tata directors, the cream of society from Bangalore, select senior bureaucrats from Tamil Nadu and all business associates of Titan. Designer and art curator Rajeev Sethi choreographed the event. Those present can still recall, silhouetted against the late evening sky on the roof of the factory, the figure of renowned dancer Daksha Sheth, performing to the sound of rousing drumbeats, accompanied by dozens of dancers at different levels. Even as the sun set on their dancing feet, it had risen for Titan Watches.

Xerxes was always fond of saying that Titan was founded in moments of serendipity, whether it was finding the right people for the right job or choosing what business to launch or making the decisions such as the one Xerxes made overnight, in consultation with Minoo Modi, to focus only on quartz watches, or setting up a plant in the state of Uttarakhand which helped the company write off some pretty large debts. This continued into the future, playing a key role at various points in the history of Titan.

TWO

HIGH ROAD TO HOSUR

It was November 1982. The advertisement in the *Times of India* only said a large business house was looking for sales executives for a job based in Bombay, but it was enough to get Bhaskar Bhat, then selling everything from almirahs to locks for Godrej & Boyce in Ahmedabad, to apply. He had had enough of the city, having spent four years there, not to mention the two years studying at the famed Indian Institute of Management, Ahmedabad (IIM-A), in the late 1970s. 'I had just got married and we were getting restless,' recalls Bhaskar, managing director of Titan Company Ltd since 2002.

It was a cool morning, at least for Bombay which is humid and hot for most of the year, when Bhaskar arrived for an interview with the consulting firm A.F. Ferguson & Co. (AFF) in late 1982. The advertisement mentioned only a French collaboration to sell some components, but what these were Bhaskar didn't know. 'Anita Ramachandran [a senior member of AFF] interviewed me and found me suitable to progress to the next stage of the interviews and that's when she mentioned that the Tatas were planning to enter into watches,' says Bhaskar, whose twinkling eyes and ready smile give away the fact that he was a fabulous mimic during his student days at IIT-Madras.

Interviews with Anil Manchanda and Xerxes Desai followed and, in a few weeks, Bhaskar found himself employed in The Watch Project of Tata Press. He was its first recruit when he joined in May 1983. Even as they awaited governmental approvals, Tata Press and France Ebauches had signed a separate sales agreement to sell its movements in India. Bhaskar would be its one-man sales force.

Earlier, Vibha Paul, a graduate of the Faculty of Management Studies, Delhi University, (who held later senior roles in PepsiCo, the Future Group and Max India) had joined TAS straight out of college and, as was the practice, done short stints in various companies of the Tata Group. She met Xerxes at the TAS interview as he was on the panel, and joined Tata Press on probation in June 1982. Xerxes promptly put her on the job of working on the feasibility report of the project.

At this stage, The Watch Project was conceptually very different from Titan as it eventually emerged. Government policy dictated that a watchmaker should manufacture at least 80 per cent mechanical or hand-wound watches. 'But we could see the writing on the wall; it made no sense to be in wind-up watches. The whole world was moving to quartz,' Vibha recalls. On numerous visits to HMT showrooms to check out the state of watch retailing, she found that 'it was like walking into a morgue with watches in their little plastic coffins, the lighting was terrible'. HMT made a small number of quartz analogue watches based on Citizen products but concentrated largely on robust wind-up watches for the Indian market. Its brands such as Sona, Sujatha, Nutan, Janata, Pilot and Rajath (an automatic) were all household names in the 1970s. 'It had become very clear: watches had to be sold as items of personal adornment, not just to tell the time,' says Vibha.

As early as 1984, Vibha managed to wangle a visit to the HMT factory, thanks to Prakash Rao, sales manager at HMT in Bombay. He was known to both Bhaskar and B.G. Dwarakanath (Dwarak), who was production manager at HMT's electronic quartz analogue watch unit. Dwarak, who later joined Titan, took Vibha around the facilities and she got a fair idea of the intricacies of watch-making. But, with no clearances in sight as yet, time moved slowly for The Watch Project even as the background work for it continued.

Vibha, then in her early 20s was made project coordinator of a huge new press being built in Nerul, New Bombay; she did this while simultaneously working on the feasibility report. Meanwhile, Bhaskar was sent to the France Ebauches factory in France a couple of times to learn how movements were made and assembled so he could assist Indian buyers of France Ebauches products. 'I can strip down and reassemble a mechanical watch,' says Bhaskar, recalling how, with a suitcase stuffed with sample movements for small-time watch assemblers, he used to travel to Chandigarh, Parwanoo (in Himachal Pradesh) and Jaipur, staying in 'hole-in-the-wall' hotels. 'We used to get a paltry commission on sales. It used to pay for my salary and travel and kept the project alive,' he says. Bhaskar remembers the harrowing time he had with trying to collect dues from a Delhi businessman to whom France Ebauches had sold movements directly. 'These guys had cleared the goods from customs but had not paid France Ebauches. So Anil sent me off to collect the dues. Every time Claude Gaudot, then heading marketing for France Ebauches [a senior industry professional and horologist], visited the businessman concerned, he would treat him like a king, getting him to stay at the Taj. He was a very decent and trusting human being, and thought he had a good relationship with them. However, they never paid up,' recalls Bhaskar.

This was when Bhaskar was becoming familiar with the watch industry in India, sellers, makers, middlemen and all. But this is not to say he was not assailed by doubts. After all, what was an IIT-Madras, IIM-A graduate doing as a travelling salesman? 'I had even gone for an interview with HUL [Hindustan Unilever Ltd, then Hindustan Lever Ltd] surreptitiously. My friends who were doing very well in hotshot, visible positions would say: "*Kya kar raha tu?!*"' With approvals still in the pipeline, there was no telling when the launch would happen. But stay the course he did.

Bhaskar's patience paid off. TIDCO's involvement with the Tatas as partners on this project propelled matters forward and once the central government gave the green signal, a little over a year from the time Bhaskar joined, things moved fast. The JV agreement stated that the chairman would be a TIDCO nominee while the operational post of managing director would go to the Tatas. The ink had hardly dried on the JV agreement when Minoo Mody swung into action. He met C.V.R. Paniker, an IAS officer who was then the chairman of TIDCO, and told him very clearly that having a political appointee as chairman would make it very difficult to function. 'I will recommend someone who will be acceptable to you but it cannot be a political appointee,' Minoo explained. He had already talked to A.L. Mudaliar who had retired as chairman of the paints company Imperial Chemical Industries (ICI) and was at the time chairman of Bata India Ltd. Mudaliar, hailing from the state himself, jumped at the idea of heading a Tamil Nadu-based company. Paniker obliged and moving tactfully, got the required approvals from the Tamil Nadu government and Mudaliar was appointed the first chairman of Titan Watches Ltd. Minoo was the first vice chairman, while Xerxes was appointed managing director.

Recalling those days, Shaktikanta Das, who was the chairman of Titan from mid-2006 till October 2008, says: 'My earliest recollection of Titan watches was when I was a deputy secretary involved with the Tamil Nadu budget. The project was approved and while making budget allocations for TIDCO – those days it used to depend on the government for equity participation – Titan watches would come up often for discussion. I recall many were curious [to know] how a new player would be able to stand in a market which was then completely dominated by HMT.'

The project cost to make two million quartz analogue watches, in 1985, was calculated to be ₹54 crore. The company was incorporated with an equity base of ₹3.55 crore which, by June 1987, had expanded to ₹17.43 crore after a successful public issue of shares. Fifty-one per cent of the equity was held by TIDCO-Tatas; the rest was with the public and institutions, such as the Unit Trust of India. France Ebauches as well as the International Finance Corporation (IFC) also invested in the equity. At present, the two promoters have a marginally higher share, at 52.91 per cent of the equity. The project also received foreign currency loans of ₹18 crore from IFC, which additionally subscribed to the company's equity to the tune of ₹50 lakh. IFC's coming on board also proved to be a long-drawn process. Ironically, the Union Industries Ministry had, in the first instance, refused to recommend the release of foreign exchange for the project. As with anything connected to finances, the first port of call for solutions was Minoo Mody, who then consulted Noshir Soonawala, the director-in-charge of finance, Tata Sons. Noshir came up with IFC as the simplest and least-cost option. He felt they were professional and would extend support to an unconventional project like this one. Indian investors would be more expensive and less understanding.

Anil Manchanda and M.N. Ramdas made preparations to meet IFC officials in Delhi. Ramdas, who had initially joined Tata Press as company secretary, later became its chief accountant. He had also played a key role in taking Tata Press public in 1984. 'Although we had promised Minoo we wouldn't raid Tata Press for personnel, in sheer desperation we asked him if we could hijack Ramdas for Titan. His brief response was: "Don't worry,

I will keep an eye on Tata Press",' recalls Anil. Ramdas came on board as general manager, finance, in January 1986.

When Anil and Ramdas presented the project to IFC's India chief, Athishdam Tharmaratnam, and his team, their initial reaction was that Titan was getting a hearing only because it was from the house of Tatas. Besides, what they were asking for was beyond the scope of the Delhi office; the proposal was, therefore, forwarded to their head office in Washington. After a series of lengthy telephonic discussions, the senior manager in Washington, Jemal-ud-deen Kassum, finally committed to bringing a team to India to evaluate the project.

Kassum was assisted by Declan Duff, a financial analyst, and Douglas Fenton, a technical evaluator. Together with Tharmaratnam, they helped the Titan team through the evaluation, assessment, approval and loan-agreement negotiations process. 'The wealth of international experience they brought to project assessment was invaluable. They looked into every aspect of our business plan, from manufacturing to sales and marketing to administration to finance. They visited our collaborators France Ebauches in France, at their own cost, to evaluate how [they] planned the technology transfer and technical training. They looked into how France Ebauches would create technical documentation in English for our staff. This level of thoroughness kept our team on its toes,' says Anil. Clarifying that as there was a foreign exchange crunch at the time, projects requiring forex were thoroughly scrutinized, he says, 'One thing I personally got to see was the detail they went into. They brought in a lot of objectivity and their monitoring was excellent so the risk would be minimized.'

After the project was evaluated and approved by the IFC team they insisted on an equity stake in the company. Only legal documentation remained a major hurdle. IFC India's legal advisers were the well-known law firm, Amarchand Mangaldas, in Bombay. However, most of the work at the Titan end was done by Anil and Ramdas with inputs from Minoo. The agreement provided for close oversight by IFC at every stage of financial activity not directly connected to operations, with particular attention to distribution of dividends and temporary or long-term lending of surplus cash.

'We negotiated long and hard but could not settle many of the contentious issues. Kassum then suggested that we come over to Washington and meet with their legal team to sort things out. Ram and I spent a week there going over, with IFC's first-rate legal team, every sentence of some couple of hundred pages of legalese. We had a daily night-time conference call with Minoo, who was very clear about what we should not concede in terms of operational freedom,' recalls Anil. Ramdas and he worked round the clock that whole week, staying up nights redrafting for the presentation the next morning. This was the only time there was a touch of the adversarial in the engagement between Titan and IFC, mainly owing to the latter's strict guidelines, with everything requiring a heads-up from 'those above'. After touching breaking point more than once, Titan and IFC finally reached an in-principle agreement late one Friday evening. True to their work ethic, the IFC legal and project team then worked through the night to polish and generate the final documents. Eventually, on a rare working Saturday for IFC, both teams went through every sentence again. It was nearly midnight when the two parties initialed the documents.

'When the final deal was done Kassum had a private word with me in his office. He thanked me for leading a successful negotiation, but added, "I don't think you made any friends out here. You left a lot of blood on the conference floor",' says Anil chuckling at the memory.

TIDCO's T.K. Arun recalls more twists in the funding story. IFC insisted that the funding body needed to be exempt from the

Usurious Loans Act dating back to the 1900s and instituted by the British to protect agriculturists. 'I had never even heard of this Act, nor could I locate it. Even our lawyers didn't have it. I searched the library at Shastri Bhavan [a government office] in Chennai and found a compendium of law which showed this Act was actually in force and had not been repealed; everyone had forgotten about it!' says Arun. However, IFC Washington, courtesy Amarchand Mangaldas, was aware of the Act. Although Indian financial institutions were apparently exempt from its provisions, nobody was sure which state government department was required to issue the exemption order to IFC. Arun approached the Tamil Nadu government's Finance Secretary: 'I told him it was urgent as we had to get the funding through. He listened to me and went through the Act and said he would get it done. He called in an undersecretary and dictated an order of exemption and signed it. Without this exemption, IFC wouldn't have given us a dollar.'

Well before the IFC funds were tied up, there had been some drama about appointing a banker for Titan. In the seven odd years of Titan's gestation, its expenses had been borne by Tata Press. Now the new company needed a full-fledged banker. This is when Canara Bank had come into the picture with its young, dynamic head, the late B. Ratnakar, playing a key role.

Back in 1984 when things began moving, Xerxes and Anil realized it was time to have a separate bank account through which they could secure an advance towards share capital and take over all expenses directly. The company was also getting to a stage when letters of credit would have to be opened to import equipment. Minoo suggested State Bank of India (SBI) since many Tata companies already had an excellent relationship with it. Besides, it had a wide network of branches, ideal for a company with a pan-India vision. Vibha was despatched to the nearest SBI branch in Prabhadevi (in Bombay) with a letter of request for application forms to start the process. However, the

SBI bank manager turned down the request saying it needed a resolution from the Titan board in order to open an account. 'Flabbergasted, I called the branch manager and said that, as with other banks, the resolution would accompany the filled application form, but he only reiterated [their] position. The next day, Xerxes, Ramdas and I were scheduled to go to Bangalore so I thought we would deal with the issue upon our return,' recalls Anil. At this time, the key technical staff was in place and Xerxes and Anil were interviewing other senior staff. 'I was spending most of my working week in Bangalore and weekends in Bombay. Xerxes was spending about two days a week in Bangalore. The West End hotel in Bangalore was our home away from home. I had a complete set of clothes permanently parked there for over a year and a half and [the hotel] used to get [them] laundered and kept ready for me,' says Anil.

The general manager of the hotel, Ashok Karumbaya, was Xerxes's friend. He made sure the Titan team was well looked after. He also often had drinks or dinner with Xerxes and Anil. During the visit following the SBI drama, the question of bankers cropped up. 'Ashok suggested we forget about SBI and talk instead to Canara Bank, a smaller bank, which was developing a reputation for service and speed. We agreed. When our office opened the next day, there were already messages from the office of the chairman and managing director of Canara Bank. Xerxes called back and Ratnakar expressed his keenness to work with a Tata company; he invited our senior management team to lunch at the ITC Windsor Manor. Ratnakar turned up with his regional manager and other high-ranking officials,' recounts Anil.

Ratnakar impressed the Titan team with his dynamic personality and good conversation; indeed, very little time was spent talking shop. That is why, as Anil recalls, 'To our utter surprise, by the time we got back to the office, which was much closer to the hotel than the Canara Bank headquarters, an official was waiting for us with the requisite paperwork to open an account, start a loan facility and initiate the process of opening letters of credit. Everything went smoothly and at a pace none of us had ever experienced before.'

As for SBI, sometime in 1989 someone from the bank's regional office in Bangalore sought a meeting with Xerxes. He suggested they meet with Anil first. On the appointed day, the regional manager and branch manager came over and expressed a desire to serve Titan in whatever capacity, as second bankers, or with specific facilities and services, given SBI's long-standing equation with the Tata Group. Anil promptly brought up Titan's experience with the bank. 'I told him that the group relationship was of no use when we needed them and that unless they changed that stance or admitted that they had wronged us, they would never do any business with Titan,' says Anil, and that's the way it stayed for as long as Anil was associated with Titan.

While dealing with funding, the team had also been working on where to locate the plant. TIDCO initially wanted the unit to come up in Pudukottai in interior Tamil Nadu but Xerxes and Anil felt the dusty terrain was unsuitable for watch manufacturing. TIDCO's other suggestions, among them Maraimalai Nagar, near Chennai, Tiruchi and the hill station of Ooty in the Nilgiris, didn't come up to scratch either. The Nilgiris, particularly, had very strict environmental laws. Hosur was the last option.

Located in Dharmapuri district of Tamil Nadu, on the border of Karnataka and only 50 km from Bangalore, Hosur was a small town with a population of barely 20,000 in the 1980s. Two large units, one for Ashok Leyland trucks and the other for Ind-Suzuki motorcycles, the country's first 100cc bikes, had already come up there but, for the most part, Hosur was virgin territory. TIDCO officials were not too keen on locating Titan there since they felt most of the benefits went to Karnataka as senior company executives preferred living in Bangalore. In the early

1980s, Bangalore still had much of the charm that had given it a great reputation: wonderful weather and plenty of green cover. The IT boom and its consequent real estate frenzy and eternal traffic snarls were a long way away. 'I first came to Bangalore in 1959 as a student. We could hire a cycle for four *anna*s [25 paise, the currency had been decimalized but old terminology was in concurrent use] in the morning and cycle all day. I fell in love with the city,' Anil reminisces.

There was another, more strategic, reason as to why Titan wanted to locate its plant in Hosur and establish its headquarters in Bangalore: HMT's watch plant was located in that city. Titan looked to HMT for expertise, given that it had created a pretty solid ecosystem for watch manufacturing. Xerxes said as much in an interview published in *Business World* magazine in December 1989: 'One reason why we chose Hosur was its proximity to Bangalore, the centre of HMT's watch operations. Based in Hosur it would be easier for us, we felt, to draw people out of HMT, particularly people with technical and managerial experience. To put it straight, we aimed to raid HMT and we did it. It turned out to be good for them and us. HMT was grossly overstaffed and promotional avenues at the top were not many.'

But the real 'raider' of HMT was I.K. Amitha who would come to play a decisive role in Titan's manufacturing expertise. In the early days, Xerxes and Anil had called on Amitha, who was then executive director at HMT and an authority on watch manufacturing. He arranged for them to visit the HMT plants in Bangalore and Tumkur (now Tumakuru), some 70 km from Bangalore. Both Xerxes and Anil were impressed with HMT's excellent equipment and Amitha's technical team.

It had been some years since that meeting when Xerxes and Anil made the sylvan surroundings of the Taj West End their base in mid-1985. The West End is set over 20 acres of woods sprinkled with rooms and cottages and today, it is perhaps one of the last large green lungs of the city. The Gulmohar Suite at the West End would be Titan's temporary office for about a year – a place where many crucial decisions would be made.

Anil recalls a visit when he fell sick and was running a temperature of 103 degrees and Amitha called out of the blue. He had rung up Tata Press and been told by Xerxes to meet Anil as he was in Bangalore. By then, Amitha had retired from HMT and wanted to talk to Anil about the new project. So, there they were: Amitha, a former HMT man legendary for his man management skills, and Anil, one of the pioneers of Titan, discussing how the former would take complete responsibility for the manufacturing side of things and handpick good people from HMT. 'Without Amitha our project would have taken much longer,' Anil emphasizes.

Once on board, true to his word, Amitha recruited his three 'musketeers' from HMT: Hari Rao, a general manager at HMT, who had only a few years left before retirement when Amitha roped him in, M.S. Shantharam and B.G. Dwarakanath, both in their late 30s. Shantharam had worked for 15 years in HMT's watch projects division, while Dwarak had worked for 13 years in assembly. They were the core members of Amitha's crack team. Vibha was charged with coordinating the setting up of the factory. 'My job was to make sure people made decisions,' she recalls with a hearty laugh. 'I kept the process going, but most of the decisions were taken by Amitha.'

The first task was identifying the right parcel of land in Hosur. 'People would show us fields upon fields and we had to decide,' she recalls. They finally zeroed in on a 15-acre plot in the industrial estate developed by State Industries Promotion Corporation of Tamil Nadu (SIPCOT), and work on the plant began.

'Those days, with hardly five or six of us around, we were doing all sorts of work, be it taking delivery of cars or hiring drivers or getting telephone lines. I would run to the SIPCOT office at Hosur almost daily and we finally took possession of the land on 6 February1986,' recalls Dwarak. The mandatory ground-breaking ceremony was performed in mid-March 1986 and a year later, by early 1987, the factory was up and running.

Meanwhile, at the West End, the excitement was building. The Bombay team comprising chiefly Xerxes, Anil, Bhaskar and Vibha, would fly down for the week while the Bangalore team focused on manufacturing. 'We used to have endless spreadsheets of calculations and I used to miscompute often. So much so that they all called me Miss Compute,' says Vibha giggling at the memory. Xerxes and Anil kept everyone on their toes. Once, when Vibha was laid low with measles, Xerxes found the time to fuss over her. 'Xerxes had the time and patience for everybody. Sometimes I felt like telling him I already had a father in Delhi!' says Vibha.

The licence issued to Titan was for the manufacture of 2 million watches – 1.6 million mechanical and 0.4 million quartz. Making mechanical watches is a complicated process as it involves a lot of components and needs a huge investment. Quartz added to the investment. But before Titan could take a decision on mechanical watches, an unexpected event worked in their favour. Rajiv Gandhi, who had become prime minister after his mother's assassination in 1984, loosened some of the strings that had been constraining the economy. Consequently, the government stopped micro-managing the industry and Titan suddenly found itself free to choose whether it wanted to make mechanical or quartz watches. In the mid-1980s, India had already been making watches for 25 years, with HMT leading the pack producing about 6 million units annually. But they were all mostly mechanical hand-wound watches or automatic self-winding watches that sold for around ₹400 apiece. A quartz analogue watch with a day-date mechanism has 70 to 80 components while a mechanical hand-wound watch has around 100 to 120 components if it is a plain three-hand watch with a day and date function. An automatic watch can have up to 200 components and requires more maintenance than a quartz watch.

The team stayed up well into the night discussing the pros and cons of mechanical vs quartz. Shantharam, Amitha, Hari Rao, Dwarak, all of them advised Xerxes that there was no point investing in mechanical watches when the whole world was opting for quartz. Xerxes heard them out patiently and knew he had to make a decision. 'Let's all go to bed now and I'll let you know in the morning,' he told the team. While they slept, he had a long conversation with Minoo, going over all the pros and cons in detail. In the morning, everybody trooped into the suite, eager and expectant. Xerxes looked around the room, delaying his announcement, keeping everyone waiting and setting them on edge. Then, he announced that Titan would not make mechanical watches, only quartz. It was a momentous decision, one that would define the company in the years to come. 'Quartz is the technology of the future,' Xerxes told his team. 'Quartz has fewer moving parts, is cheaper and easier to make and maintain, it's lighter and slimmer, and it's right by the consumer.'

Once the decision was made to go quartz there was a flurry of action. The entire plan was recast and the machinery required was re-examined. This time Hari Rao and Shantharam were dispatched to France and Switzerland to finalize the machinery required in consultation with Jacques Robert, the technical director of France Ebauches. They decided to opt for Swiss equipment for the more complicated, precision machines, and source the lesser accuracy equipment from HMT.

The report prepared by France Ebauches had envisaged Titan manufacturing all the watch movements over a seven-year period. 'I was aghast to see this part of the report. I felt this was ridiculous. I told them we can't invest ₹20 crore in the first year and make parts only worth ₹20 lakh. I said we have to compress this whole thing as time was of crucial importance,' says Hari Rao. And that's what they eventually did, making all the components needed for watch movements in three years flat instead of seven. Way ahead of the phased manufacturing programme that Titan had committed to the Directorate General of Technical Development!

Claude Gaudot was a key member of the Indo-French collaboration. He had been hired by Titan in 1985 when it became clear that the Titan project was about to take off. His primary job was to be the contact person and facilitator for commercial as well as technical communication and exchanges. Claude was very well connected to the watch industry in Switzerland, France, Germany and the United States, having also worked for Timex, the largest brand in the US. 'More than anything he was a very fine gentleman and became our good friend and guide. He personally guided and supported all our engineers who went to France Ebauches for technical training,' says Anil.

Some time in 1987 he accepted Titan's offer to join them as general-purpose advisor, mentor and guide, at the level of vice president. He and his wife, Alice, moved to Bangalore. 'I don't think we made a trip to Europe ever after his joining us, not guided or not accompanied by Claude. It became natural to turn to him when we wanted to acquire some equipment or technology or designers or spare parts and sure enough he would find the right person or company for us,' recalls Anil. Claude was literally a man for all seasons. It was he who found a person in Switzerland to evaluate the designs of Titan's first slim movement in 1993; which went on to win a design award from the Department of Scientific and Industrial Research (DSIR) in 1996. He identified designers and marketers for Titan's Eurowatch project and, later, when Titan went into jewellery manufacturing, most of the gold processing equipment and technology was sourced from companies Claude located and introduced. Titan's alliance with Timex, though shortlived, would not have come about if Claude had not introduced Anil to Lawson Campbell, the acting chief executive officer of Timex in India.

While the factory was being set up, recruitment went on for the watch-making unit. Although Titan had made a commitment to the Tamil Nadu government to generate employment in the state, the challenge was to find hundreds of workers with the aptitude for intricate watch assembly. Amitha decided to start by scouring schools in smaller towns and villages for likely candidates: they had to be over 16 years old and had to have passed the class 10th exam. 'We didn't want anybody whose minds were already bent out of shape by the ITIs; we wanted fresh minds. We sent teams of people to small towns; young boys and girls were given attitude and aptitude tests. If one hundred applied, around three got selected,' says Xerxes. Amitha, based on his experience with the Japanese – Citizen was HMT's technical collaborator and Amitha was trained in Japan and could even converse in Japanese – introduced a psycho diagnostic test (PDT) to gauge the ability to engage in repeated work. 'Amitha would join me and my team along with the HR team to visit schools to conduct the PDT as well as check for dexterity in the use of their hands,' recalls Dwarak. The 40-strong recruitment team started with schools in Hosur and then moved on to other towns.

S. Deenadayalan, a human resources executive with Titan at the time, recalls the arduous process of meeting with principals in district schools and convincing them that good jobs were at hand for their wards. In the first batch, around 60 teenagers were signed on before the recruitment process scaled up. But there were problems: this was the first time the chosen young people were leaving home. Many had not even travelled to other towns. Something had to be done to help them cope. So, Titan set up transit homes with foster mothers and fathers to take care of them. It was also decided that only one person per family would be recruited. As Dwarak explains: 'We would take care of that one employee, and he or she in turn would have to take care of their family and the education of their siblings.'

The bright-eyed and garrulous Amodha is one such recruit, one of five selected from a school in Pondicherry (now Puducherry) back in 1989. It's been nearly 30 years; she now works in the cases assembly unit. 'We were from a poor family, my father was a building contractor and my mother was an ayah in a school. I initially wanted to become a nurse. But I was very proud that I got a job even while I was studying and people in my school encouraged me to take it up,' she says in a conversation at Titan's Hosur factory. Lokambal too joined the company in 1989 after she finished school. She is from a small village an hour's drive from Namakkal in Tamil Nadu, some 250 km south of Bengaluru. Her father ran a teashop; he was an alcoholic. 'We went through a lot of hardship. We were three children; my father found it difficult to educate us. For the first two years after I got the Titan job, my father kept insisting that I return to the village. He wanted to get me married to a relative. But I was very stubborn about holding this job and standing on my own feet. Our hostel warden convinced him about the job, prospects, safety and the fact that it was a Tata company. So, he eventually accepted my working here,' she recalls.

Dealing with a young workforce from rural Tamil Nadu came with its own baggage. 'There was one incident, almost like in a Tamil film,' recalls Deenadayalan. 'One of our employees, a young girl who was forcibly married off to her cousin, came to us for help saying she wanted to get out of the marriage. The husband's side came with henchmen to take her back but she refused to go. I didn't know how to deal with this situation. But I said, cinema-style, if you remove your *thali* [mangalsutra], you can stay, and she actually removed it and flung it across to them. Then I told them that I'd have to inform the police since the girl was under 18 [years of age]. The marriage was annulled.'

Titan has not been only about watches and, later, jewellery. From its outset, Titan has been widely recognized for the employment it provided to the differently abled in its plants in Hosur and Uttarakhand. While seeking employees for non-hazardous operations, managers were pointedly asked why the differently abled could not be recruited. Such measures resulted in the number of such employees on its rolls significantly increasing and exceeding the minimum mentioned in the Persons with Disabilities Act. In later years, Titan's initiatives were acknowledged by the Rajiv Gandhi Foundation and the National Centre for Promotion of Employment for Disabled People.

Besides the employment of the differently abled, Titan's corporate social responsibility (CSR) initiatives have earned several laurels including being the first recipient of the Loyola Institute of Business Management's Mother Teresa award, as also awards from FICCI, the PHD Chamber of Commerce and Industry and the Rotary.

In early 1988, when the ceremony to dedicate the plant to the nation was being planned, Xerxes and Anil discussed the need for a commemorative motif. Since it was neither a foundation-laying nor an inauguration ceremony – the factory had already been producing watches for nearly a year – a traditional plaque would look odd. Xerxes suggested installing a sundial. The idea appealed to Anil. 'Each sundial is specific to a geographical location and has to be adjusted to the day of the year to yield correct time. But no one in Titan knew how to design one and we did not know where to look. That weekend I was talking to Kusum, my wife, and remarked how funny it was that we were making such sophisticated watches and had no clue about designing a sundial. She promptly said, "Why don't you ask Radha?"'

Embarrassed that he had not thought about it himself, Anil immediately called Radha – Professor Venkatraman Radhakrishnan – a renowned radio astronomer and member of the Royal Swedish Academy of Sciences. He was professor emeritus and director of the Raman Research Institute, Bangalore, with which the Manchandas shared a compound wall. Radha's wife, Dominique, and Kusum were friends. 'We went across to see him and I made my request for help. That is how it came to be that the successor to Nobel Laureate C.V. Raman helped us create a steel-plate sundial which was executed in brushed steel by a Bombay workshop with help from Sudhir Diwan who designed our corporate office and our first few showrooms.' This sundial still stands in the watch division at Hosur.

But let's wind back to early 1987 when the factory was ready to roll, people had been hired for the shop floor, the marketing team was in place, and Titan was readying itself to launch its watches.

THREE

TITAN WATCHES START TICKING

It was a cool morning in 1987, 23 December to be precise, when a motley bunch of Titanians congregated at Safina Plaza, off Bangalore's hip and happening Commercial Street. There was a nip in the air but Xerxes was in shirtsleeves as usual, unmindful of the chill. Others such as Bhaskar, who was the all-India sales manager, Anil, Amitha, Hari Rao, Ravi Kant, the vice president of sales and marketing, Bijou Kurien, the regional manager for Calcutta, C.R. (Raghu) Menon, general manager, sales, and others from the manufacturing and marketing teams, milled around. The occasion was the inauguration of Titan's first exclusive store by Chairman A.L. Mudaliar. In keeping with local custom, a pumpkin was smashed outside the store for good luck, an *aarati* was performed and the store was declared open.

Safina Plaza was not, and still isn't, a mall, but it was Bangalore's first stab at organized retailing. Curious onlookers, other retailers, members of the watch trade, all came to visit the store in the shopping complex which overlooks a central courtyard. The Titan showroom, in the care of manager G. Kannan, certainly stood out. The show window displayed a large quartz crystal in the centre of a stand of Titan watches, reinforcing the technology that Titan had plumped for. Around 165 watches were on display, with their prices up front for all to see. On launch day, the company ran half-page advertisements in the newspapers showing each watch with its price printed below, like a catalogue, creating quite a stir among the public. Therefore, when the store opened, potential customers came clutching the newspaper clipping to point out exactly which watch they wanted to buy. 'It was the most modern showroom in Safina Plaza and in addition to customers, there were representatives from other brands and watch retailers who visited,' recalls Bijou, a long-time Bengaluru resident.

This showroom went on to inspire other top brands to open outlets in Safina Plaza even as Titan itself experimented with lighting, window display and counter arrangements. What was perfected in this store would be rolled out in Titan's aggressive franchisee-led retail plans. The sales team, led by Bhaskar, was very excited. 'As sales guys, we really liked the advertising; people [walking in] with paper cuttings of our ads [gave] a boost to our brand. This was unique in the Indian landscape at that time,' he says.

Although the official launch was in December 1987, Titan had started distribution through the existing watch trade as far back as April of that year. Even then, it had been clear that it needed to create a special shopping experience for customers. Existing retailers were making huge profits but they were not willing to invest to upgrade their showrooms. The thinking was that anyone who wanted to buy a watch would come to the shop regardless of what it looked like. At least that's how it had been when HMT ruled the roost. 'We, on the other hand, wanted to make it a pleasure for customers to shop and to also pull in passers-by who did not have watches on their shopping list. We wanted to encourage ownership of multiple watches by enticement. We decided to go into direct retail, which wasn't part of the original business plan, to help understand the game and to see if we could change it and encourage other retailers to modernize too,' explains Anil.

Safina Plaza was still under construction at that point. Haji Sattar Sait, the proprietor of the mall, saw the potential when Titan offered to take the store next to the main entrance. Karam Oberoi, Titan's administration and human resources head at the time, had located the property. It was a risk because the happening retail places such as Commercial Street and Brigade Road were barely a stone's throw from Safina Plaza. 'However, the location helped allay the fears of big watch retailers in the main shopping areas. We decided to keep the first showroom small and assured retailers that we would share all the learnings from our little experiment. Later, we took the adjoining shop, then the one above it and still later another two shops to serve as a service centre. Titan thus became an "anchor store" for Safina Plaza,' says Anil. It remains one of Titan's best-selling stores in the country.

Titan launched with five watch collections: Exacta (steel), Fastrack (sporty models for youth), Classique (gold-plated dials with leather straps), Spectra (two-tone – steel and gold) and Royale (gold-plated dials with gold-plated metal bracelets). The lowest priced was Fastrack at ₹350 and the highest was Royale at ₹700. From day one, Titan was projected as a premium brand and it quickly achieved market leadership.

The Safina Plaza store was designed by Mumbai architect Sudhir Diwan who had also designed Titan's first office in Bangalore. He was recommended by renowned architect Charles Correa whom both Xerxes and Anil had worked with in CIDCO and who had developed the master plan for the Titan township in Hosur. Sudhir had never designed a showroom of this type before, so he took a trip to Switzerland and France to see what was happening there in contemporary retailing.

Everything about the Titan stores was different: their finish, layout and design. Mood windows were reflective of the range on display and their sales staff kept an eagle eye on customers to see if they were stopping to peep in or were missing the store completely. Those who entered were encouraged to browse; they were not hustled to buy. Lighting proved a challenge: illumination from the roof was not effective because more than 50 per cent of the light bounced off the glass counters. It took designers time, imagination and experimentation to come up with fixtures and fittings at different angles to alter the incidence on the counter surface and to perfect the lighting under the glass. 'Other consumer-goods marketers, including top garment brands, came to see our showrooms and drew inspiration from them. More than anything else we were the first to establish that investment in creating a pleasant shopping experience pays. Many of the new brand outlets went on to use our franchise agreement as a model,' recalls Anil.

That first day at Safina Plaza, the showroom sold 17 watches; the first month's sale was 313 watches. The Classique range was easily the bestseller, accounting for around 65 per cent of the total sale. The Spectra range was a flop and was swiftly dropped. In-store research showed that people did not even linger over the two-toned beauties that Titan's designers were so proud of. The ability to let go of things that didn't work was a strong corporate ethic and helped create the brand that Titan became, says Anil. 'We regularly dropped products that did not [match] expectations. Expensive failed initiatives included a major departure in our advertising style sold to us by a fresh VP inductee into O&M. We went with a style we had considered and rejected earlier and developed a typical jingle and a slogan – "The changing face of time". It didn't work and we quickly dropped it. Letting go quickly meant that the consumer [and] the employees did not have time to absorb and retain mishaps associated with the brand,' he explains.

But the months leading up to the April 1987 launch were manic, recalls Vibha. 'We tore apart style magazines and put together the various looks and styles we wanted and then literally went around the world – Switzerland, France, Taiwan and Hong Kong – mostly to find what we were looking for. The appearance parts of a watch: the case, dial, hands, strap, were all available with multiple and widely dispersed suppliers so it took us some time to bring things together.' Travel was usually done in teams: Vibha and B.N. Yallamalli, the technical expert in watch design when shopping for appearance parts; Amitha, Shantaram, Hari Rao and Dwarak when watch-movement technology was involved, and generally with Xerxes or Anil when business decisions needed to be taken.

With no watch designers around, Vibha and the team used their own ingenuity to work out designs from supplier samples. 'We would pin up the sample of a watch case, with two or three dials beside it, pin the strap next to it. We used one board for each design and the first time we showed it to suppliers, they were quite bewildered. We had so many reiterations for each design; Xerxes would be the final arbiter,' recalls Vibha. Although many people provided logistical and technical support, the watch collection was basically put together by Vibha and Xerxes who worked extremely long hours and on countless weekends, recalls Anil. Foreign travel too was a pretty arduous affair. The RBI sanctioned a mere $100 (₹1,300) per day as foreign travel expenses. 'Moreover, I would go with suitcases [full] of watches and had to declare them, and people would look at me like I was a smuggler,' recalls Vibha with a chuckle.

Initially, Xerxes said, it was a mix-and-match operation. 'In Hong Kong, suppliers would lay out their dials and bracelets and we would match this dial with that bracelet, or that colour; we did all kinds of things. The first designs we launched were all put together in Hong Kong, with modifications we asked for. It was a humble beginning but there was no other way; there were no watch designers in India,' explained Xerxes. It was only later that Titan began hiring art and design graduates from the National Institute of Design (NID), taking them to the international watch fair in Basel, Switzerland, and to look at stores in Paris, London and Geneva. 'We gave them a thorough exposure. I was also learning,' said Xerxes. 'I knew something about art as much of my life was spent in aesthetics, in printing and in designing hotels, but I knew little about watch design.'

Xerxes's strong sense of aesthetics and attention to detail would come to drive Titan's watch-and-store designs. 'He changed the paradigm of retail for us,' says Bijou. 'We initially looked to HMT showrooms or stores of other brands. But Xerxes told us we should look at showrooms of Western countries as models to emulate. He put pressure on us to create stores that conformed to international standards.'

Raghu has an interesting, if embarrassing, story to relate regarding the initial batch of Titan watches. It was December 1986 and Raghu was setting out for Bombay when Xerxes told him, 'Raghu, please stop by at Bombay House and give J.R.D. a watch from our first batch.' Raghu duly did so. A fortnight later, Raghu was again in Bombay and he decided to call on J.R.D. to check on the watch. Imagine his shock when J.R.D. returned the watch saying, 'It's a quartz watch, isn't it? It is not working, take it back!'

A stunned Raghu immediately called up Xerxes and all production was stopped. A thorough check revealed that one particular batch of batteries had been on the shelf for too long; such batteries tended to make the watches go slow or stop working altogether. That's when Titan realized the importance of fresh batteries and the need to monitor their shelf life. It was surely the ultimate irony that J.R.D. received the one watch that was defective!

Glitches aside, the next stage through which Titan's watch project had to pass was sales and marketing – crucial for any successful business. Here, too, a few people would come to play a key role in the direction that Titan would take; a couple of them have since passed away. One was Anil Gore who played a significant role in the screening and selection of the ad agency, O&M. He also guided the sales and marketing team. Ravi Kant had worked with Gore in Hawkins and had been recommended by him. More importantly, Gore would set Titan on a path of market research and validation before all major decisions on marketing-and-communication strategy were taken. 'Xerxes thought it was a waste of time and money but went along because we were planning to commission Tata Economic Consultancy Services. In our first decade, many of the initiatives ascribed to brilliant insights were, in fact, a gift from smart researching of what customers would actually buy, as also the when and why, rather than what they said or what we as a company thought,' explains Anil.

The other person who was instrumental in laying a strong foundation for sales and distribution was Raghu, to whom both Bhaskar and Bijou reported. He had joined Titan in interesting circumstances. One fine summer morning in 1986, in the Mumbai office of air-conditioner maker Voltas, a Tata Group company, the head of the profitable appliances division got a call. The caller asked, 'Is that Mr Menon? This is Minoo Mody from Tata Sons.' Minoo then went on to explain how the Tatas were starting a new watch company in Bangalore and were looking at internal Tata candidates for the position of general manager, sales, and Raghu's name topped that list. Would he be interested? Raghu recalls being flown down to Bangalore where the largest interview panel he had ever faced quizzed him in a room at the Taj West End. There were about 15 interviewers, including the entire board of directors of Titan and several from TIDCO as well!

Raghu laid the foundation for the CFA (carrying and forwarding agent) structure and dealer network which formed the backbone of Titan. Top business persons in various Indian cities were appointed CFAs; to this day they remain part of the Titan family. Those chosen were people of impeccable integrity and values with a strong sense of ethics. Raghu, who was passionate and aggressive about the brand, recalls his brief to the regional managers: 'All towns in India with a population of 10,000 should have at least one Titan dealer.' Thus, it came to be that even a town curiously named Margherita in Assam had a Titan dealer!

Another individual who advised the Titan team initially was Vinod Bali, an executive director of Tata Chemicals and very well regarded in the Tata Group for his commercial acumen and expertise. An unassuming but consummate professional, he guided discussions on sales policies and structures with a sure touch.

Over multiple strategy sessions with senior members of the Titan management and Vinod, Raghu finalized a sales policy for Titan Watches Ltd. It was decided that Titan would deal directly with the retailers since all existing distributors were beholden to HMT. Titan would supply only against advance payment, a practice unprecedented until then, to ensure that retailers' cash was tied up in Titan stock. Advance payments would make for more congenial and efficient sales visits because a salesperson would not have to start the call with the unpleasant task of reminding the store owner about pending payments. In spite of initial resistance even internally to the idea of 'no credit to dealers', Raghu recalls putting his foot down on that decision and insisting that that was the only and best way for Titan.

This was an extremely unusual policy stand and many from other industries were sure it would not work. But work it did, and in spades; in fact, it was one of the biggest contributors to Titan's initial financial success. Later, the sales staff made many attempts to get this policy reversed, promising a dramatic increase in sales. 'But I always opposed it vehemently and successfully on the grounds that what was being promised was deliveries and what the company needed was cash flow,' says Anil.

The seeds of the franchisee model were also sown in these early sessions. Titan proactively attracted business persons from outside the watch trade to set up watch shops even if they needed extra help to do it. Partly because there were no middlemen, Titan could also offer better margins to retailers. 'All these policies served us well in the initial years; they were the key to maintaining low working-capital borrowings and enabled us to show profits from the very first year of operations,' says Anil.

HMT was different; it followed the traditional distributor-led model. Distributors fed the watches to the retail trade and controlled the channels as well. Watch showrooms and retailers were typically located in the older, more congested parts of town. While Titan couldn't afford to ignore the large retailers, it decided to take the watch showrooms to where potential customers flocked. Ravi Kant, who had come from Kinetic Engineering, makers of two-wheelers, says they sensed, and research later confirmed, that the customer profile was changing. People were willing to spend on good-looking watches; they were also willing to own multiple watches, even though ownership of multiple watches was still low then. 'At that point in time, we estimated that 17 per cent of people owned nearly 40 per cent of the watches sold,' says Ravi. This figure came from the regular-usage-and-attitude studies that Titan commissioned every two to three years either through IMRB or Quantum Research. The study also threw up data on ownership of watches.

Ravi and his team had discussions with many potential retailers: book stores, jewellery stores and even restaurants, referred to as

NTOs or non-traditional outlets, which contributed greatly to the sales. 'I remember in Coimbatore we talked to the owners of Annapurna restaurant, famous for its dosas and crowded all the time. We set up an outlet right next to it,' recalls Ravi. Titan even talked to the Bata chain of stores, thanks to Mudaliar who was also chairman of Bata India, when Global Chairman Thomas Bata Jr was visiting Bangalore to set up a shop-in-shop counter, but that venture didn't take off. Meera Harish (then Gopalakrishnan), a young management trainee, recalls lugging a watch counter up the stairs of Gangarams, a well-known book store on MG Road in Bangalore, to interest book lovers in Titan's watches.

'Location was paramount,' says Ravi. In order to build the franchisee network, Titan engaged with young businessmen with no background in retailing, leave alone watches, to set up outlets that their spouses could run. 'I personally visited the first 40 franchisees to see the location of their stores and explain the model to them,' says Ravi. Of course, store openings were not without their share of drama. Meera recalls the opening at Abids, a shopping district in Hyderabad, by actor Poonam Dhillon, fairly well-known then. Xerxes, who was present at the opening, hadn't even heard of her and had to be given a full briefing after which he carried on an extensive conversation with her!

Titan's initial success owed much to its dedicated franchisees. Some such as Raja Upalapatti in Visakhapatnam, Prabhu and Jogu Prasad in Vijayawada and M.K. Dattaraj in Bengaluru have been with Titan right from its inception. S. Nagarajan, initially the head of Titan's businesses in western India, spearheaded much of the franchising operations. One such pioneering franchisee is C. Shivakumar. Shiv runs Prabha Engineering, a successful auto-components unit in Chennai making parts for truck-maker Ashok Leyland, among others. Shiv's family owns and runs a department store, Puniamoorthi Pillai Department stores, in Thanjavur, Tamil Nadu.

Shiv put up a Titan Watches counter at his store. But selling them wasn't easy, he recalls. HMT was right on top and people didn't understand what a quartz watch was. They came into the shop, admired the watches, asked for HMT and left. 'People didn't want to buy watches at a department store – they only wanted to buy them at a watch store,' recalls Shiv. Bijou advised him to go ahead and stock HMT as well. 'If you feel you can sell HMT, stock both; if you keep HMT you will get more walk-ins for Titan as well,' Bijou told Shiv.

Shiv's early association with Titan was not without drama. Titan watches were stolen from his store, not once but twice. The first time round, a full 100 watches were gone – and they hadn't been insured. The second theft occurred a few months down the line. 'The police caught the thief and recovered the watches. I met the thief in the station, a tall, muscular fellow. I asked him why only Titan, not HMT. He grinned and said that he hadn't intended to steal; he had missed the bus to Pudukottai [a nearby town] and ended up stealing as he had time on his hands. And he stole Titan because they were higher priced,' Shiv recalls laughing at the memory. Today, he owns over a dozen stores, ranging from World of Titan outlets to Tanishq and Gold Plus showrooms and Titan Eyeplus outlets.

Titan had a fine set of regional managers to anchor sales. There was the savvy Avi Ahluwalia for the north, the shrewd C. Srinivasan for the south, the retailing brain S. Nagarajan for the west and the dynamic Bijou for the east (followed by Jayashree Mohanka, a brilliant quizzer and champion of the *Economic Times'* popular Brand Equity Quiz). Titan also had a bright set of sales executives and officers across the country, many of them personally interviewed by Raghu and Ravi Kant. Raghu recalls how Ravi would ask: 'How much is 7.5 per cent of 23,000?' or 'How much is 12.5 per cent of 85,800?' and so on because he believed sales officers had to have good numeric and quantitative abilities in order to effectively book orders from dealers.

Meera recalls how the sales team dreaded Ravi's 'market visits' because he would cross-examine them not on percentages or watch sales but on how much the Raymond store across the road was selling per month or what was the market share of Bata in this market or how much the market share of Onida was in the electronics store next door and so on. He was obsessed with the need for the sales team to be aware of marketplace dynamics.

Titan's sales team soon learned that while the great-looking watches were flying off the shelf in the cities, in the hinterland they didn't cut much ice. Raghu and Bijou were looking for opportunities to expand sales territories. They had heard that Tata Tea in Munnar, a small town in the Western Ghats in Kerala, was planning a hefty bonus – two months' salary – for the festival of Onam. 'Why don't we hold an exhibition of our watches in Munnar during this time to generate some good business?' Raghu told Bijou. So off they went, armed with 1,000 watches, two to three from each model of the 165 Titan had launched. They flew to Cochin (now Kochi) and travelled by van to Munnar.

They took a space at a store near the famous High Range Club of Munnar, in the middle of picturesque tea estates. 'We expected a lot of people to come on the first day but hardly anyone came; we sold only three watches. We were really surprised,' says Bijou. They put up posters announcing the sale in the housing colonies and made announcements via a loudspeaker. The following day they sold five watches! By the weekend they had sold only 32 watches. 'We decided to go to where the workers were and loaded our watches into an ambulance and travelled with it all over. But even that was a failure. The workers told us that as soon as they received their bonus, it was time to repay their debts. And they didn't need watches as their lives revolved round the estate bell: the first to get up, the second to report for duty, the third for lunch and the fourth to go home,' says Bijou. It was a chastening experience.

Bijou says the learning was that even though people in smaller towns and rural outposts had money, it didn't mean that watches were a priority for them; they were more intent on clearing loans and perhaps buying jewellery. And, consumers from rural pockets preferred to travel to smaller towns nearby to make, what was for them, larger purchases. The company's sales in smaller towns picked up when it launched the lower-priced Sonata watches in the late 1990s.

Another time, when Raghu and Bijou were analyzing the town-wise sales of Titan watches, they discovered that Moreh in Manipur was selling watches in high numbers. So they decided to pay a visit to unravel the secret behind the unusual 'success'. Moreh is on the India-Myanmar border and most of the watches were being bought and sold in Myanmar. This probably seeded Titan's subsequent idea to launch its watches in the entire SAARC (South Asian Association for Regional Cooperation) region comprising Afghanistan, Bangladesh, Bhutan, Nepal, the Maldives, Pakistan and Sri Lanka, rather than be limited to India.

In a short period of time, Titan had cornered 55 per cent share of the quartz watch market in the country. HMT was caught leaden-footed as the market began to move from mechanical to quartz. In an interview in *Business World* magazine in December 1989, Xerxes said, 'Our rivals are resorting to all kinds of tactics to stop their market shares from contracting. HMT has been reduced to making consignment sales and has started paying more by way of commission. Worse, the company is constantly cautioning watch retailers not to stock our brand. If we had done the same thing we would have been hauled up under the MRTP [Monopolies and Restrictive Trade Practices] Act.'

HMT failed to respond with aggression to the Titan juggernaut. In an interview to *Business World* published in January 1991, K.S.

Gergan, then an executive director at HMT, conceded that Titan had identified the gap in HMT's product line and said being in the public sector hampered its response. 'Our handicaps...are that we have to operate under rules, regulations and procedure. The attitude towards work of a typical public-sector employee is sadly not as keen as in the private sector. Lastly, the government is not always helpful to us,' said Gergan.

Malavika Harita, who works with advertising agency Saatchi & Saatchi Focus, was with the marketing department of HMT in the mid-1980s. She had joined the company fresh out of IIM-Bangalore and spent six-and-a-half years there. She recalls how she used to chafe at the marketing blunders HMT made. 'Titan went directly for the fashion route,' she recalls, 'and I think that's where we sort of lost out because they started selling the watch as a fashion accessory and we were selling it as your papa's watch or mama's watch or as a legacy thing and as a timekeeper to the nation. But people stopped looking at the watch as a timekeeper.' Titan, she says, exploited every single mistake that HMT made. 'They had range, they had fashion and I remember that I used to hear that Xerxes Desai himself was the brand custodian. That was the attention to detail they paid to the whole fashion thing and I think that's basically where HMT lost the plot,' says Malavika.

A critical decision Titan made early on was to set up a service network alongside the showrooms. Earthy and earnest H.G. Raghunath (HGR), who had also joined Titan from HMT, spearheaded the service initiative. A year after the showroom was opened at Safina Plaza, Titan added a service centre above the showroom. HGR says the company recognized that service was often identified with some shabby back room; Titan wanted to change this paradigm. 'Quartz was new, and there were worries about the battery. Just like we started selling watches in air-conditioned showrooms, we set up similar service centres where customers could sit and wait comfortably while their watch was getting repaired,' explains HGR. Dealers themselves were encouraged to open service centres, with subsidized watch-repair kits provided and staff trained by Titan. 'My advice to the service centres was: Don't make a fortune of a customer's misfortune. We had to change the impression that often service is looked upon as a rip-off,' HGR explains. Xerxes added, 'It was all about repair the watch, repair the damaged relationship, repair the company's reputation.' Besides, this would allay customers' apprehensions about getting quality replacement batteries. Clearly, many of them had had bad experiences with smuggled watches which were often fitted with substandard batteries in the unorganized after-sales service market.

Titan had successfully negotiated the tricky business of sales and distribution by working out an effective franchisee model which cut out middlemen and offered retailers a slightly better margin that it labelled as a cash discount. Titan offered no credit and even today, it maintains a cash-and-carry system with dealers. This worked to the advantage of retailers because the more Titan watches they sold, the more money they made, and with their own money invested in the business, retailers too gave sales a push. The Annual Report for 1987–88 bears this out: by the end of the first year of launch, Titan had sold 3.44 lakh watches. Success had come in double quick time.

FOUR

THE MAGIC OF MOZART

Mani Ayer strode into Roda Mehta's room at the Ogilvy, Benson & Mather (OBM) office in Bombay. 'The Tatas are going to make watches to compete with HMT and we've been asked by this new company, Titan, to make a pitch,' he said. It was typical Mani, succinct and to the point. Mani, who took over the ad agency as the youngest managing director of the global group's affiliate in India in 1969 at the age of 34, had been at the helm for 17 years now and had earned a formidable reputation. Founder David Ogilvy described Mani as 'the most outstanding individual in the Ogilvy network'.

The year was 1986 and Titan was thinking ahead. Its technical team was in place, work was apace on the factory building but much depended on its advertising and marketing game plan. Ravi Kant had not yet joined the company, so Titan did not have a marketing head. Anil Gore gave of his time unstintingly for the Titan launch; Vibha Paul, who had no hands-on experience in advertising, suggested books and other reading material to Xerxes and Anil Manchanda so they could educate themselves about the arcane world of advertising. But that was not enough; they needed to get professional help, and quickly.

Guided by Gore, the Titan team started the exercise of choosing an agency and devising an advertising strategy that would create a lasting brand akin to those of classic watch brands worldwide. After a thorough selection process, OBM was chosen over the likes of Lintas (now Lowe Lintas), Rediffusion (now Rediffusion Y&R), and Chaitra (now Leo Burnett), all of whom tried very hard to win what promised to be a high-value account. In OBM's favour was the fact that the creative head, Suresh Mullick, the head of media planning, Roda Mehta, and Mani himself would be directly and personally responsible for the brand. Mani's exact words, Anil recalls, were, 'If you call and ask for the account manager for Titan, you will be connected to me.' This was a huge commitment from one of the largest and most respected agencies to an as yet unborn brand.

Mani kept his word. He and his team devoted enormous amounts of time to Xerxes and the young Titan team and, in the process, also exposed them to advertising as a craft. There was much to-ing and fro-ing between Bombay and Bangalore (where Titan set up its headquarters) before even the first word was put down or the first visual floated. Mani was a strategic thinker, good with money matters and managing people. He and Xerxes hit it off immediately and, 32 years on, O&M (as OBM was rechristened in 1989) still remains Titan's agency. Mani and Xerxes are both no more but their initial strong rapport sustained the bond.

When it started off on the Titan campaign, OBM had nothing to go on: the watches were still a long way from being made, and all the agency had was a concept of French quartz watch movements with attractive dials and cases from Hong Kong. HMT had an 80 per cent share of the legitimate watch market and a formidable reputation as *the* Indian brand, literally owning the mechanical-watch category, which was a lifetime purchase and prized as a hand-me-down to be treasured.

'What we get from our agency can never be better than the inputs we provide,' Gore told Xerxes and Anil and insisted Titan give the agency a written brief. Vibha created the first brief with many inputs – and much interference, it must be said – from Xerxes and Anil. It was drafted and redrafted several times. But it seemed to pay off as, 'according to Mani, this was amongst the best written briefs he had ever seen. At that time, we thought he was just being polite, but experience has shown that he was probably right,' says Anil.

The 1970s were a tumultuous period in India's history: the Bangladesh War of Liberation in 1971, followed by the Emergency between 1975 and 1977. This resulted in engendering a low-income, low-savings society. Things had begun to change in the mid-1980s after Rajiv Gandhi became prime minister. The restrictive economic climate began to ease up and consumers slowly became more confident and aspirational. An environment evolved in which Titan's philosophy of watches as a fashion statement would resonate with consumers. Titan was in the right space and at the right time. 'Titan ventured to change mindsets by suggesting that if you could change your clothes every few years, you could also look at adding a new watch as an accessory,' explains Roda as we chat in her gracious apartment in a leafy enclave of Pune.

The next few months saw the OBM team tirelessly and endlessly debating various approaches to brand-building and communication, in terms of content, layout, design, strategy and delivery. Coffee flowed freely by day and Scotch by night as meetings carried on into the late hours. Day-long meetings were held either in the OBM conference room or at the Tata Press office near the Siddhi Vinayak temple in Dadar, Bombay.

Xerxes, both Anils, Ravi Kant and Vibha represented Titan while Mani, Suresh, Roda and Jaideep Samarth, the account director, represented the agency.

The basic premise was that the competition was the smuggler, not HMT or Allwyn, both of which had a minuscule presence in the quartz watch market. Smuggling gangs had access to the best the world had to offer from Switzerland, Japan, Taiwan and Hong Kong. They kept the market flooded with the latest models and had gained a degree of confidence amongst customers.

The other issue OBM had to grapple with was the use of the Tata legacy in communication. While the brand denoted trust, it was of little consequence in the consumer space for it was not aspirational in image. The only consumer-goods company in the Group then, TOMCO, sold mass brands such as Hamam bathing soap and 501 bar soaps (later sold to Hindustan Unilever). It was the agency's considered opinion that the Tata brand name could not project the aspirational image that Titan wanted, though the sense of trust it denoted was an important factor.

Roda, a management graduate of Jamnalal Bajaj Institute of Management Studies who had trained in the UK in research and account planning, proposed in-house executed brand-positioning research. Consumers stratified across sex, age, income, education and population strata categories were asked to score a battery of statements on two primary dimensions for a watch – importance and uniqueness. For example: 'This watch gives accurate time' was seen to be important but not unique. 'This watch comes in a wide range of international designs' ranked medium on importance but very high on uniqueness. 'This is a quartz watch with battery replacement' ranked low on both importance and uniqueness.

The results of this survey laid the foundation for the strategic direction of Titan. The first point was that a world-class watch and watches in a wide range of international designs were clearly differentiators. The second was that these attractive watches had to be affordable. The third was that the Tata name offered the consumer a strong assurance of trust. So the brand positioning developed for Titan was: 'A world-class watch in a wide range of designs and prices brought to you by Tatas.' This was debated intensely within the agency – looking at all the nuances from the perspective of brand brief, the competitive landscape, the target consumer profile, client expectations and aspirations – before it was finally adopted. All communication for the brand, whether in print or on television, would close with 'Titan Quartz from Tata'.

It was now up to Suresh Mullick and his creative team along with a young art director, Andrea Pereira, to develop the advertising campaign. Those were anxious days, full of anticipation and excitement as the team waited with bated breath for the magic to be spun. After cogitating over many days, Suresh called for the OBM team to meet. He spelt out that Titan's launch advertising would have no models and no celebrities; the watches would be the heroes. Using a colour catalogue format, the full-page advertisement would mention the price under each design. The prices spoke for themselves as offering excellent value. The idea of displaying pictures of the watches was to showcase the range and the variety, and to make the point that such products had not been seen before in India. There would be two such print ads created featuring some 15 or so distinct watches each. The headline was designed to draw attention to the international collection from an Indian brand. There would be minimum text in the advertisement. Further, the ad had to serve a double purpose: one, sell to the customer looking for a quartz watch and two, convert someone who was looking at a traditional mechanical watch into a quartz watch customer.

Xerxes and Anil responded favorably to the brand direction the agency suggested and the creative presentations; all that remained was consensus on the text, its wording, font size and typography. 'When we created the advertising, we didn't have a product in hand, we were going by what was in their minds and what they were trying to create,' recalls Roda. The half-page ads that eventually appeared in newspapers were an absolute reflection of what they had learnt from the positioning research, she says. The launch ads enabled potential customers to do their window-shopping at home and then walk into the store waving the day's newspaper, pointing out the watch they wanted to buy. This is exactly what happened, as the Titan team saw at the inauguration of the Safina Plaza showroom. It was a masterstroke to have the price up front in print. Readers saw a smart-looking watch and immediately got the answer to the obvious question, 'How much?'

'We at the agency believed strongly in the brand. All of us working on the brand bought the watches – some of us more than one! That was the real proof of the concept: that owning more than one watch could be a reality,' says Jaideep.

Xerxes, being the expert on printing after years with Tata Press, was very particular about the quality of the pictures of the watches to be reproduced in newspapers and magazines. He would spend hours on the proofs with Ravi Jasra, the colour picture processor who supplied the materials to publications for printing. 'He wanted the watches to look as good in print as they did in real life. A virtual impossibility then, given the technology,' says Jaideep. But, the Titan ads came pretty close, recalls Anil.

As punctilious as Xerxes was, Ravi Kant was more so. Meera Harish, who had joined Titan as a management trainee, recalls being in Ravi Kant's room along with the OBM team as he obsessed over the ads; checking to see if the watch code mentioned alongside each item looked better aligned to the left or the right and doodling away to get it right. 'The agency kept waiting patiently till he finished, not daring to interrupt his thinking! I was on a flight from Bombay to Bangalore later that week and the first thing I did when I got the day's paper at the check-in counter was to see if the ad had appeared fine with all the little product codes! I was relieved and elated to see our first full-page ad,' says Meera. This full-page ad appeared in May 1989.

The next move by OBM was in television advertising. Xerxes was a creative person with a keen eye for detail, language and aesthetics. He was a Western classical music and jazz aficionado, and in Suresh Mullick he found the perfect collaborator. Suresh, too, had a keen ear for music, both Western and Indian classical, as all his work revealed. He had made several landmark short films for Doordarshan in the 1980s such as *Spread the Light of Freedom* featuring the country's top sportspersons running with a torch, and the famous *Mile Sur Mera Tumhara* featuring India's top musicians. He was also the brain behind Cadbury Dairy Milk's successful relaunch campaign in 1981 with the line 'Sometimes Cadbury's can say it better than words'. Best of all, Xerxes and Suresh shared a great rapport.

In order to derive maximum synergy, it was decided that the television ad would be an adaptation of the catalogue-style print ad. It was an easy decision to make the watch the hero and showcase Titan's entire range. The big question was what soundtrack should accompany the visuals. A commonly used audio track was to offer a product description, but this was ruled as being too boring and likely to detract from the visual. The second most popularly used track was a jingle. But the success rate for jingles was under 5 per cent. Also, jingles needed to be translated owing to the linguistic and cultural differences across regions, and that made it a challenging task. No one had managed to do this effectively.

After much discussion, it was agreed that a catchy piece of instrumental music would work best. Here again there were many choices: Indian pop music or classical music were considered and dropped because they did not have universal appeal. That left Western pop or classical. Eventually, they decided upon a piece of Western classical music with mass appeal. Xerxes and Suresh were well placed to make the right choice, given their knowledge and affinity of Western classical music. Suresh zoomed in on Mozart's 25th Symphony, and picked the track from the 1984 award-winning movie, *Amadeus*, on Mozart's life. Jaideep had picked up the CD for him while holidaying in London. So confident was Suresh that he had a scratch television ad prepared and presented it to the Titan team as an almost finished product. Xerxes immediately liked what he heard of Mozart and decided this was it. He had made his choice. The campaign was proposed and approved in its entirety in one sitting.

The first television ad showed a series of watches one after another. As the second hand ticked, the watch face changed. The ad conveyed the message that you didn't have to go abroad to buy a quartz watch anymore; you could buy it in India. This television campaign was a seminal achievement that defined Titan for the next 30 years.

It was unheard of in the mid-1980s to use Western classical music for an Indian brand aimed at an audience little exposed to that genre of music. But it struck a chord. Xerxes felt the music gave the brand a world-class feel. 'Of all the symphonies of Mozart, this one has a tremendous amount of enthusiasm and spirit about it,' Xerxes would say. Titan's signature tune would go on to entrench itself so deeply in the public mind that television audiences knew it was a Titan ad the moment the music came on even if they weren't watching. Subsequent ads used many variations including Indian musical instruments to essay the symphony. As Xerxes said with a chuckle, 'I don't know if Mozart will turn in his grave or get up and applaud with the kind of things we've done to his symphony using so many other instruments.' Mozart's 25th Symphony remains Titan's signature tune to date.

Many man-days went into picking and choosing colour schemes for outdoor branding, product packaging, letterheads, visiting cards and dozens of other points of Titan interfacing with the rest of the world. The campaign released to wide acclaim from customers, the watch trade and even advertising professionals, and effectively harmonized across different media, from newspapers and television to outdoor and in-shop advertising.

Sanjiv Khamgaonkar, a film-maker who worked with OBM as creative director in the initial days of Titan's advertising, has high praise for the decision to show the watches like a catalogue. 'The key thing was to get people to say "Wow!"' he explains as we chat at a Café Coffee Day outlet right opposite the teeming Siddhi Vinayak temple. Round the corner is where it all started – the Tata Press office. Sanjiv's family lived down the road from this office and Xerxes had once bought a painting from his father, a painter of repute. A few years down the line, when Sanjiv quit OBM to strike out on his own as an ad film-maker, Xerxes was to commission him his first film for Titan.

Sanjiv, who worked with ad film-maker Radhakrishnan Nair of Magic Eye Films in the first series of catalogue ads in print, says they used double exposure (repeated exposure of film to light) techniques to shoot the watches. 'We got some beautiful details because of the double exposure,' he says. 'We used some *jugaad* to keep the watches up straight; we used metal tongue cleaners that we could twist to prop up the watches; pasting the strap on to the tongue cleaner would give it a spine. We spent days shooting the watches. Xerxes was very demanding.'

The self-taught Radhakrishnan, known among his colleagues as Radha, who has made at least 25 films for Titan, says there weren't many doing watch photography in the mid-1980s. Sometimes it would take almost a whole day to set up the lighting as a stainless steel bracelet watch would need different treatment from one with a leather strap. 'Nowadays with digital, you can shoot everything separately and put it together; those days we used to struggle. Xerxes said the full-page ad should look like it was bringing the showroom alive in the newspaper. He said the watch had to be shown in its actual size in the newspaper so that consumers knew exactly how it looked,' explains Radha in his small studio-cum-office off Bengaluru's busy MG Road. There was no doubt the advertising campaign played a big part in Titan's successful launch. The company's Annual Report for 1987–88, its first full year of operations, says Titan earned ₹19 crore and sold 3.44 lakh quartz watches. Xerxes Desai, in his report, acknowledges the role of the agency in this success.

The next step in Titan's advertising game plan was to encourage a repeat purchase of watches. Till Titan came on the scene, a watch was a lifetime purchase; you bought one for keeps. Titan's advertising thrust, thus, turned towards offering more reasons to buy watches. This resulted in a series after the launch campaign that presented the watch in the context of similarly priced consumer items. There was one, for instance, with the tagline, 'Next time she asks for a sari, get a Titan instead!' Titan was competing with a large grey market of cheap Hong Kong- and Chinese-made watches. Therefore, as Roda explains, 'The context of the advertising, the product quality, the music all made Titan feel like an upper-end product. But the sales force constantly wanted to make it a lower-end product so that it could compete at the base end, which is when new ranges of products began to be conceived and introduced with sub-branding.'

By the late 1980s, sales were ticking along at a good nip. With Titan watches now fairly well known, Ravi Kant, who felt the catalogue approach had run its course, wanted a different approach to the campaign. It was a fact that whenever a watch was featured in a print ad, sales of that model spiked. However, pre-deciding on the watch design by a customer could also be counter-productive as that could lead to dissatisfaction if the store did not have it in stock. Also, the general feeling was that it was time to 'humanize' the brand; it was time to market Titan more aggressively.

However, Titan and OBM had another more pressing issue to contend with: strained ties. The strain, recalls Ashok Sarath who was creative director with the agency in Bombay, began in late 1988 or so. While Titan's top brass had set up office in Bangalore, the agency handled the account from Bombay and the advertising lost a lot of its freshness. 'There was pressure from Titan to make the advertising more "hard-hitting" and rational as in trying to get mechanical watch buyers to convert through a rational message. There was also the cost and speed of running the business from Bombay that seemed to be weighing on both the agency and Titan, and there seemed to be a feeling that the client was dictating matters and the agency wasn't coming up with something fresh,' explains Ashok.

As a way of overcoming the servicing issues, one of the agency's star account managers, Vijay Bhat, and one of its leaders, Chintamani Rao, were shifted to Bangalore to handle Titan and Brooke Bond, another big client based there. The issue was to deliver a creative product that would raise the bar and also offer a quick turnaround. A subsidiary task was to build bridges at every level and improve the relationship between Titan and the agency. Though the management issues had been fixed, it fell to the creative product to be the saviour, since that was Titan's key concern. 'This was when Mani Ayer told me, over several drinks, that it was up to me to make sure the business did not go from our hands. I moved to Bangalore in July 1989 as creative director and inherited a department that was gutted – one art director, one visualizer-trainee [who] later became one of the city's most awarded and respected creative directors, Manmohan Anchan, and a copy trainee,' recalls Ashok.

In 1989, Titan was gearing up to launch a new range of plastic watches branded Aqura for college students and young adults. One of the key concerns for Titan was whether the agency, now renamed O&M, was up to the challenge. That was the task

Ashok was vested with: to come up with a great idea to show that the ad agency still had the zing. 'We took them through 14 concepts and then finally narrowed down on one. This involved a black-and-white shot of someone hiding their face with the hand they wore their watch on. At the bottom of the ad were the colourful watches. The tagline was, "Get ready to get noticed,"' explains Ashok. It was also the first time people were used in Titan's advertising.

The idea of showing people in black and white and the watches in colour, as in the print ad, resulted in something sophisticated and fashionable that gave the advertisement high visibility. 'It got us the credibility with Titan that we needed at that point,' recalls Ashok. Titan's faith in O&M's creative abilities was restored. The first six months had been disastrous at a personal level for everyone, recalls Ashok. 'No time off, no rest. But on a professional level, the results were quite satisfying. We were no longer under threat of getting the sack and the relationship became quite solid at every level,' he says.

Titan had always invested in conducting massive amounts of research to understand who buys, why they buy, who decides, who goes to the shop, who pays, and for what occasions they buy, and they studied the results to plan their products as well as their ad campaigns. One of the points that emerged from this research was that people were increasingly gifting Titan watches to friends and relatives on significant occasions in their lives. Titan decided to capitalize on this finding. 'So there were these nice films that were scripted and made which focused on the emotions of receiving and giving a Titan watch as a gift. The basic idea was to capture the moment of gifting, [with the attendant] emotion of being gifted something so special,' Ashok explains. This theme became an entire advertising campaign by itself. It could be a gift for entering high school or college, getting engaged or married, starting a job or getting promoted or retiring, and so on, explains Anil. All ad campaigns were tested, either pre- or post-release or both times, on small focus groups. The television ads that resulted for the gift theme showed a husband gifting his wife a watch, a daughter gifting her parents watches, a young man presenting a watch to his girlfriend. The one that worked brilliantly was the husband gifting his wife. The tagline was 'Rediscover the joy of gifting'. This tagline would remain a leitmotif in Titan ads for many years.

The first set of films in this series were scripted by Aruna Nair and shot by Mahesh Mathai, a talented film-maker who had once been Anil's neighbour in Bombay. The series was a huge hit, recalls Ashok. The husband presents the watch in a restaurant, and upon his signal, musicians play the Mozart tune. The wife dissolves in tears of joy. The commercial tugged at the heartstrings and set the tone for succeeding films. In fact, in 1995, Titan used the same couple to record a similar ad for a discount sale but this time, the husband doesn't stop with presenting one watch but ends up presenting four to five, throwing the musicians into total confusion. Titan sales burgeoned that season: clearly, the film was effective. Ashok recalls Xerxes making one of his pointed observations regarding one of the films set in a restaurant; the card attached to the Titan gift box read: 'To my dearest wife'. 'To which Xerxes asked us, "How many wives does he have?" [What Xerxes meant was that it would have been sufficient to say "To my dear wife".] It was a lesson in English for all of us!' The agency hastened to change the line.

In the early 1990s, film-maker and celebrated cinematographer Rajiv Menon who had earned critical acclaim for his camera work in director Mani Ratnam's movies, *Bombay* and *Guru*, shot a Diwali promotional ad for Titan at Prasad Studios in Chennai, which featured two relatively unknown people. It was Aishwarya Rai's second television commercial (her first was for Pepsi, which also featured Aamir Khan); and it had a young musician called

A.R. Rahman adapting the Mozart melody. The ad featured a husband and wife (Aishwarya), with the latter finding a Titan watch on the bed as she is getting dressed. This ad too did well for Titan over the Diwali shopping season.

But the big breakthrough for Rajiv and Titan was the ad showing a father gifting his daughter a Titan watch at her wedding. 'What was interesting was that the ad captured the change that was taking place in India then. The change was that it was not mother and daughter, it was father and daughter, actually two daughters. There was this debate about whether there should be a mother at all in the film. I think this is where Titan was very brave,' says Rajiv.

'So here you had the younger daughter playing the piano – at a traditional Indian wedding – and the bride discovers the Titan watch kept by her father on her dresser. So in a way it was bridging the gap between the Western and Indian ethos in terms of emotion,' recalls Rajiv. This ad did extremely well, and Titan remained with the gifting theme for several years. In September 1992, Roda moved to Bangalore to head the agency's southern operations. The following year, Ashok moved to Delhi and Ramesh Ramanathan, a musician in his own right, was brought in as creative director from the agency's Madras office.

C.K. Venkataraman (Venkat), presently the chief executive officer of jewellery brand Tanishq and who has spent 29 years in the company, was Titan's ad manager in the early 1990s and pretty much at the centre of all the initiatives for the television commercials. A fitness enthusiast who cycles 20 km from home to the Titan office near Bengaluru's Electronics City every day, he explains that when Titan began working on the gifting campaign, it did not foresee the power of the idea; it was more a market development effort. The thinking was that if Titan could show that its watches made a good gift, it could create demand. 'That's how we saw it then. Then we felt that since our watches were not cheap at ₹500–₹700, big money in those days, they would be gifted only to close relations or friends. So we created those close-knit situations in our ads. Then we moved to marriages. Then we realized the power of this idea as it became the central theme of Titan films for quite some time,' elaborates Venkat.

It wasn't till year 2000 that Titan used its first celebrity in its commercials. This was none other than actor Aamir Khan. 'We wanted to use Aamir because of his exclusivity as those days his movies used to come out only once in two-three years and you didn't see him on TV shows and ads. So we caught him at the right time. He was also regarded as a thinking man's actor so he was the right fit for Brand Titan,' Venkat recalls.

The Aamir Khan series worked well for Titan and recall was high. Working with the selective actor also had its moments. For instance, in 2005 Aamir had just finished shooting *Mangal Pandey: The Rising* in which he had played the role of Mangal Pandey, a soldier who by attacking the British set the Sepoy Mutiny (or the first Indian war of independence) in motion. He had grown his hair and beard for the role, a look he liked. Titan aired one ad with him wearing this look. Aamir's next film was *Rang De Basanti*, for which he had to be clean-shaven. Venkat was all for the clean look and, at a meeting with him, creative director Piyush Pandey of O&M (he would later become chairman) and his brother Prasoon, who was shooting the ad, tried to push Aamir into shaving his moustache and beard and trimming his hair right away. 'Aamir told me that he liked his look and found it cool and wanted to retain it for the next [ad] film as well. Piyush and Prasoon then agreed that we should go with the long-haired look and not with the crew cut I was suggesting. So I went along with them much against my wishes,' recalls Venkat.

A few weeks later, a big packet was waiting for Venkat. Inside was a black-and-white photo of Aamir shot by ace photographer

Atul Kasbekar, who was also Aamir's manager then. At the bottom of the photograph, Aamir had written: 'Venkat, do you still want me to cut my hair?' 'The ad had been released and it was a very successful campaign, and by then I realized that they were right and I was wrong. Aamir remembered the conversations we had had and sent me this photo,' recalls Venkat with a laugh.

Titan would go on to use many celebrities for its ads: it signed on cricket captain M.S. Dhoni for its brand Sonata, and Jaya and Amitabh Bachchan for Tanishq. Some of its ads were made by film-maker R. Balki (famous for films such as *Paa* and *Cheeni Kum*), then working for the ad agency Lowe Lintas. Titan's ads would go on to bag many awards and played no small role in Titan's immense marketing success. Even though at times the company and the agency felt fatigued by Titan's signature tune, research showed that the public loved it, and so Titan has stuck to it, with some tweaks, for over 30 years.

While agencies fancy themselves as brand custodians, Roda says Xerxes was the true brand steward of Titan. 'Xerxes set the standard and epitomized all that the brand stood for. His eye for detail was exemplary, whether in the advertising or in the marketing. The big ideas were his and everybody deferred to him,' says Roda. Xerxes breathed and lived the brand.

Till the early 1990s, Titan had enjoyed immense success. Accolades had poured in for its smart-looking watches, endearing advertising and unconventional marketing methods. However, hubris would impact future decisions. The rest of the 1990s would be a period of intense struggle, a consequence of strategic blunders and misplaced ambition.

FIVE

MISADVENTURES IN EUROPE

It was the early 1990s. More than four years had gone by since Titan had stormed the Indian market and won accolades and awards for its designs, slick marketing and sparkling advertising. Sales for watches were zooming and Titan was in clover, but Xerxes Desai was restless. Now that Brand Titan had firmly ensconced itself in the Indian market, he craved more. He wanted to take Titan global.

'We believed a European launch would be good for the brand, and good for the Tatas. We had a manufacturing operation in watches which was equal to the best, so why not expand the market and also bring in the honour and the glory for Brand Titan,' said Xerxes, sitting in his spacious living room well appointed with antique furniture and recalling the old days 25 years later. While the idea to make and export watches simmered for a while, Titan began to manufacture jewellery for the European markets, precipitated by the need to generate its own foreign exchange to import machinery and components for its growing watch business. Also, as Xerxes reasoned, in the UK and European markets, watches and jewellery were sold by the same retailer, very different from the situation in the Indian markets where there were separate channels of trade for them. India had a natural advantage in exporting jewellery due to its cheap but highly skilled labour.

However, Titan realized early on that it would have no market in Europe for branded jewellery unless it built a high-end brand, so it mostly sold to large retailers and wholesalers in the UK, the US and a few in Europe. It was an arduous process for a newcomer to break into the supply chains, competing with other jewellery exporters from India and other countries, recalls Vasant Nangia, who headed Titan's European operations from the UK for a while. 'The whole cycle – from design to sample to delivery – had a lot of learning for Titan, as international buyers were demanding, [and they were] used to a [certain] level of service and product quality, not to mention sharp pricing,' says Vasant.

Meanwhile, Titan had been exhibiting its watches at the World Watch & Jewellery Show in Basel every year in the pavilion of its collaborator, Frances Ebauches, at no cost either for space or resources, thanks to the generosity of its chairman, François Perret. However, as soon as Titan revealed its planned watch project for the European market, the Swiss organizers came down heavily on the French company and forbade it from displaying anything not actually manufactured commercially in its own facility in Europe. Not discouraged by this, Xerxes came up with a plan for watches; it was something no Indian company had attempted until then. He wanted to hire European designers and create watches especially for Europe. With Indian labour cost advantages, he felt that Titan could sweep the market.

However, as Anil points out, being a high-cost watch producer at the time, Titan was at a disadvantage. 'Despite knowing my negative assessment of the situation, Xerxes insisted that I take charge of setting up the export-oriented manufacturing facility for watches; he would take over when it was time to market the product abroad. I agreed, and thus started our European adventure,' recalls Anil. Titan had already achieved initial success among Indian expats in West Asia; the goal now was to get Europeans interested in buying the brand. That apart, there were also plans to launch in the Asia-Pacific region.

Titan had to plan carefully for its European launch. In 1992, Titan launched a small operation in the UK with its India collection to test the waters. Unfortunately, these watches with their gold plating and dials did not cut much ice. Wrists were also larger, so the learning was that watches for Europe had to be designed differently. Thus was born the 'Euro Watch Project' for which a new plant was set up at Hosur to make high-quality cases and bracelets. Foreign designers were hired to fashion watches to suit European tastes and a London-based advertising agency, Lowe Howard-Spink, was hired for the campaign. 'We set up an office in London in the premises of Tata Ltd, right at Grosvenor Place, overlooking the Buckingham Palace grounds. It was posh and befitting our grand scheme,' recalled Xerxes. The intention was to unveil the range simultaneously all over Europe: the UK, France, Germany, Spain, Austria and the Netherlands, among others.

A centrepiece of Titan's Europe strategy was to acquire an important Swiss watch brand, Gerald Genta, because that would open several doors for them. But Xerxes and Anil knew they would face stiff opposition from the Swiss, who were aware that Titan was part of a big group with deep pockets. 'They were worried that something like what the Japanese had done to them would be done to them again by an Indian company. But that was a grossly exaggerated fear,' said Xerxes. In the 1970s, the Japanese had developed cheaper and more accurate quartz technology. This helped them crash the prices of watches and dominate the market with inexpensive ones. Switzerland's mechanical watch industry could not withstand this onslaught and throughout the 1970s Swiss watchmakers shut shop. It was only in 1983 that Nicolas G. Hayek, a Swiss entrepreneur of Lebanese origins, led the Swiss rejuvenation in quartz watches with the introduction of a global blockbuster brand, Swatch.

Gerald Genta was a luxury brand created by its eponymous founder, a brilliant designer who had earlier worked for marquee brands such as Patek Phillippe and Omega. When he decided to set up on his own, Genta bought a Swiss factory to produce elaborate movements and exquisite and complicated watch pieces inlaid with diamonds and other precious stones. Xerxes loved these watches. In his words, 'We really liked what we saw. Gerald Genta was making watches only to special orders. He was not into mass retailing, and was present in a small way in a few shops in Paris.' He had made classic timepieces for buyers such as the King of Jordan and the Sultan of Brunei. The price Genta was asking for was 40 million Swiss francs (₹80 crore at the time), a huge sum for Titan, despite its deep pockets. Genta wanted to scale up his distribution but did not want to be a mass brand; the understanding was that Titan would provide the front-end retailing for Genta's designs; Genta himself would continue to work with Titan and design watches. The fly in the ointment was that a key to the company's success was Genta's personal charisma and relationship with key customers, but investing big money on the goodwill of one individual was a risk.

Xerxes's grand obsession to acquire Gerald Genta had an unlikely fallout, one that would create ripples in the company. By 1990, Titan had occupied the upper end of the Indian market, but by international standards its products fit into the lower-middle range. In 1992, Titan had started work on its Euro Watch Project and the jewellery project for export. As work progressed on the manufacturing facilities for these projects, it

The Titan founding team at the Taj West End, October 1985. From left: Anil Manchanda, R.C. Hari Rao, the French translator, M.S. Shantharam, B.G. Dwarakanath, Jacques Robert (project head from collaborators France Ebauches), I.K. Amitha, B.N. Yallamalli, Xerxes Desai (then managing director), Bhaskar Bhat and Vibha Paul Rishi.

Intense planning in progress at the Taj West End, October 1985. From left: Vibha Paul Rishi, Xerxes Desai, B.N. Yallamalli (behind Desai), I.K. Amitha, M.S. Shantharam, R.C. Hari Rao, Jacques Robert, B.G. Dwarakanath, Anil Manchanda and the French translator.

Bhaskar Bhat (extreme right), who would be the future managing director of Titan Company Ltd (then Titan Watches Ltd), joins the team during its planning session.

Product finalization and review at the Taj West End, March 1986. From left: Xerxes Desai, Anil Gore and Anil Manchanda.

Bhoomi puja at the site of the Hosur factory, Titan's first watch-manufacturing plant, March 1986.

The watch factory coming up; the civil work was completed by early 1987.

TIDCO Chairperson Ms E.V.K. Sulochana Sampath visiting the factory site, June 1986. Seen, representing Titan, are (from left, walking alongside Ms Sampath) Anil Manchanda, Xerxes Desai and Hari Rao.

The third Annual General Meeting (AGM) of Titan Watches Ltd and the first to be held in Hosur, 22 December 1987. The previous two AGMs were held in Madras.

Dedication of the Hosur watch factory by Tata Group Chairman J.R.D. Tata, 11 March 1988. Also in the picture are TIDCO Chairperson Ms E.V.K. Sulochana Sampath (third from left) and Xerxes Desai.

t the dedication
remony of the Hosur
ctory, 11 March 1988.
om left: Xerxes Desai,
inoo Mody, J.R.D.
ta, François Perret
resident, France
bauches) and A.L.
udaliar (Chairman,
tan).

J.R.D. Tata and A.L. Mudaliar unveil a plaque at the ceremony.

The Hosur factory premises just after operations began, 1989.

Watches being assembled at the Hosur factory.

J.R.D. Tata inaugurating Titan's first Mumbai showroom in Colaba, 1989.

Titan's one millionth watch is released by Chairman A.L. Mudaliar, 10 April 1989. To his left are Vice Chairman Minoo Mody and B.G. Dwarakanath. Xerxes Desai is standing on the extreme left.

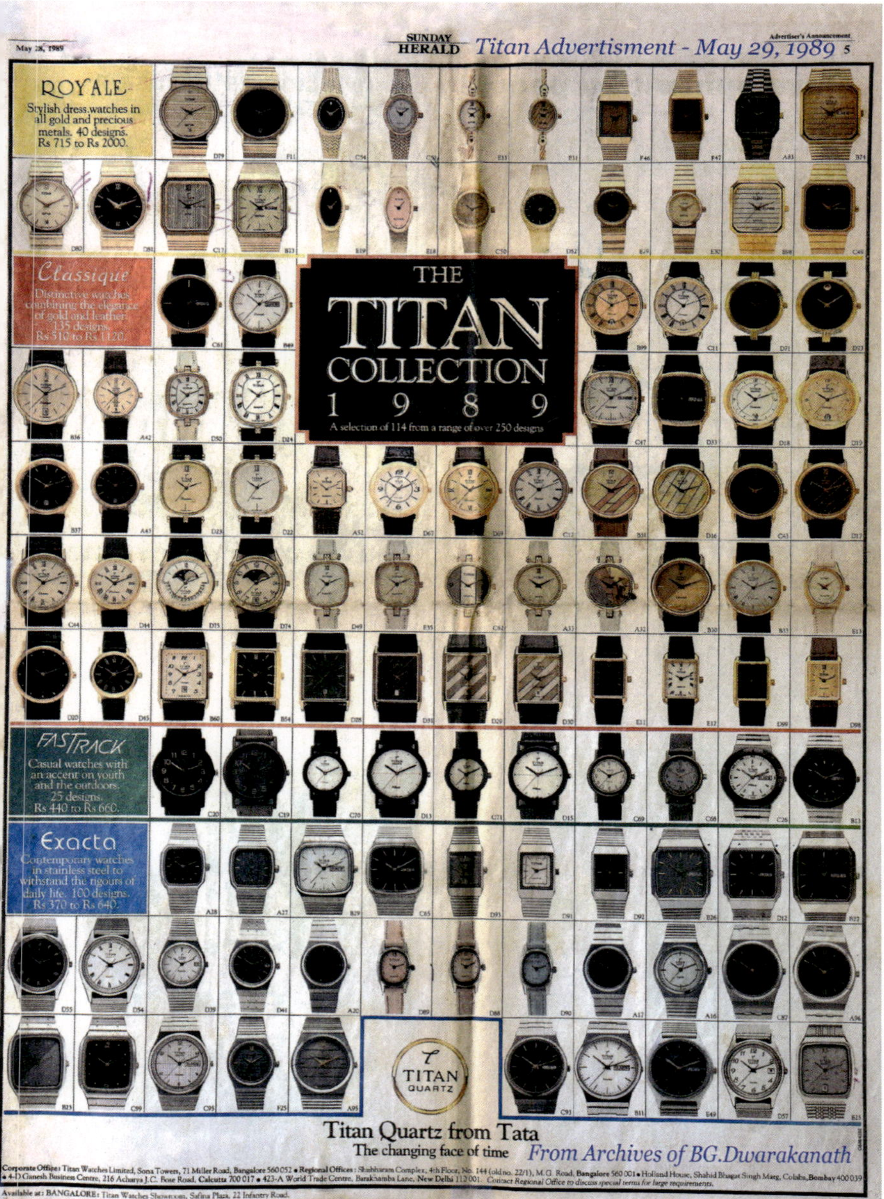

Titan's first full-page advertisement in print media showcasing its watches released, May 1989.

J.R.D. Tata inspects a machine developed by Titan at the inaugural of the watch case plant, 9 March 1990.

J.R.D. Tata with Y. Okomotho, senior vice president, Citizen Watch Co., being shown around the watch case plant, 9 March 1990. Also in the picture are Jayanti Prasad, then head of public relations, Titan, and Xerxes Desai.

Actor Kamal Haasan inaugurates a flagship store of Titan in Chennai, 18 June 1990, as Xerxes Desai and S. Ravi Kant, then head of retail at Titan, look on.

R.C. Hari Rao displays some watch components to Tata Sons' Chairman Ratan Tata on his visit to the Titan factory in 1992. On the left is I.K. Amitha.

Xerxes Desai inaugurates Titan's jewellery plant in Hosur, 19 March 1994.

Ratan Tata (centre) and Bhaskar Bhat (fifth from left) with the Titan Watches & Accessories team. From left: Ajoy Chawla , Revathi Kant, H.G. Raghunath , N. Kailashanathan, Harish Bhat, M.S. Shantharam, C. Srinivasan, Ronnie Talati, S.D. Gopalakrishnan and B.S. Prakash. Titan received the sustained excellence award at the JRD QV Awards event from Ratan Tata at NCPA, Mumbai, 29 July 2009, when the company crossed 650 points in the Tata Business Excellence Model (TBEM) assessment.

Bhaskar Bhat, managing director, unveils the new Titan logo, 28 August 2013. The company name also changed to Titan Company Ltd.

Inaugural of Titan's 1000th store in Indira Nagar, Bengaluru, 15 December 2013. From left: Rajeshwari Srinivasan, Suparna Mitra, Ajoy Chawla (second row), H.G. Raghunath, Bhaskar Bhat, C. Srinivasan, Ronnie Talati and S. Ravi Kant.

Relaunch of the first-ever Titan store in Safina Plaza, Bengaluru, 10 September 2016. The store first opened in December 1987.

A Fastrack showroom (above) and one of Taneira (below). Titan continues to reinvent the retail space with their imaginative showroom displays geared towards creating a unique shopping experience for their customers.

Titan has been known for its path-breaking advertisements. Above are stills from the 2013 'The Joy of Gifting' campaign that depicted a retiring college professor being gifted a Titan watch on his last day of work. Titan's signature tune, Mozart's 25th Symphony, continues to be used and refreshed by the company till date.

was agreed that Anil Manchanda would concentrate on the new projects and be available for Indian operations as and when his services were required; accordingly his designation was changed to executive vice president (international operations). This was the first indication that Xerxes was serious about Titan's global play.

Technically, Anil recalls, he was supposed to call the shots for the overseas operations, but in reality Xerxes ended up taking the decision on the jewellery consultants to be brought on board, as well as on the appointments of heads for the UK market, which was the base of the Europe operations. This didn't go down well with Anil. 'We started talking to Gerald Genta but did not have even a rough action plan for that company's takeover or operations. Halfway through, by early 1993, we had not engaged in any serious market studies or research other than what was fed to us by technical consultants, who earned more the more they could get us to spend,' recalls Anil.

On 4 June 1993, Anil recalls Xerxes dropping into his cabin casually one day to announce that he had fixed up a meeting with J.R.D. and other senior directors to raise funds for the Euro Watch, jewellery export and Gerald Genta projects, and as executive vice president, Anil should make the presentation and answer their queries. Says Anil: 'This was the very first big step he had ever taken in our over two-decade long association without consulting me in advance. I refused to do any such thing and, after consulting my family, informed him the next day that I would like to leave.'

Taken aback, Xerxes asked Anil to rethink his decision. But Anil had made up his mind. He did not attend the meeting with the Tata directors although he was in Bombay. From early August 1993, Anil went on leave but remained on the payroll of Titan till end-March 1994. After that Xerxes and he met only rarely. Sadly, it was a sour end to a close professional and personal relationship of many years. In a letter to Titan's chairman A.L. Mudaliar and the company's vice presidents and general managers, and copied to the directors of the company, Xerxes acknowledged Anil's outstanding contribution to Titan and Tata Press and said his departure had come at an awkward time for Titan.

However, Xerxes soldiered on with Mission Gerald Genta. J.R.D. too was upbeat about a possible takeover of Gerald Genta and called for a meeting at Bombay House with the directors of Tata Sons, recalled Xerxes. He and his team made a presentation, but they were to be disappointed by the response. Nani Palkhivala, the well-known legal luminary who was a senior director at Tata Sons, said the project made no sense for Titan as Genta made watches for only the very wealthy. Ratan Tata, who was by then the chairman of the Tata Group, seconded him. One of the senior directors said that the Tata ethos was not to 'sell baubles to the rich', while another director, Darbari Seth, said it didn't look like the right thing to do in the face of opposition. J.R.D. then became uncertain about how to proceed. Xerxes and his team also began to have second thoughts, particularly as it would have been quite an expensive buy. Much to Xerxes's chagrin, the plan to acquire Gerald Genta, whose exquisite designs had so appealed to his aesthetic sensibilities, was dropped.

Nevertheless, Titan's Europe plans were still on course. However, more problems were in store. To its surprise, it was discovered that the brand name 'Titan' was owned by an Andorran company for key markets in Europe and that Titan had to buy the rights to the brand in these markets. The alternative was to start with a new brand. This was not an option. After all, Titan had a reliable product, it had made designs to European tastes and had planned a campaign created by the London-based ad agency, Lowe Howard-Spink. However, the project was hobbled by the lack of funding. Interest rates were high in India and the company had already invested heavily to push the project. Besides, there was no further infusion of equity as partner TIDCO said it did not have the money to invest; it was also reluctant to dilute its stake in the company.

One of the key players in Titan's overseas foray in the early years, Vasant, who would go on to head the Asia-Pacific region for the Fossil Group, joined Titan in 1986 from Indian Hotels, where he was involved in project management. Fed up with living in Bombay, he too had jumped at the opportunity of working in Bangalore. Initially, Vasant worked with Shantharam and Dwarak to set up the assembly plant. Later, given his finance background, he joined Ramdas in the finance department. 'I started handling the finance part of the international operations as Xerxes was keen on Titan becoming a global brand. We set up Titan Dubai, then Titan Holdings in the Netherlands and then Titan International Marketing in the UK and that's how I got more and more involved. One fine day, Anil said why don't I move to the UK and handle operations as well,' recalls Vasant. He moved to London for three years to shepherd the brand after Titan found that the people it had hired in London had mismanaged matters. 'We found them less than honest and not willing to part with the knowledge they had of the UK market on the basis of which we took decisions in India. They made a hash of it and finally we had to sack them and make a fresh start,' said Xerxes.

Two groups were formed: Vasant, based in London, spearheading the operations and the marketing, and a former head of Seiko in Europe, Jacques Mayer, based in Paris, overseeing the design team. Jacob Kurian, who would spearhead the Tanishq revival much later, headed international marketing, based in Bangalore. Over the next year, they set up distribution in about 12 countries across Europe, apart from which distributors were appointed in Germany, Austria, Denmark, France, Benelux (a group comprising Belgium, the Netherlands and Luxembourg), Italy, Greece, Spain and Portugal.

Alongside a pan-European distribution network came the rollout of Titan's advertising campaign. In the 1990s, 'Made in India' was not quite the tag to have on products targeting European customers. So, the beautiful Titan print ad campaign had female models of multicultural ethnicity with the headline, 'No one country could have made faces this beautiful' and a tagline: 'French-Swiss-Indian-Japanese' (cueing French design/movements, Swiss steel, Indian manufacturing and Japanese batteries). The ad was splashed in popular glossy magazines across Europe: from *Vogue* to *Cosmopolitan* to *Elle*, it was everywhere. And with it was drowned millions of dollars in pursuit of the audacious dream of trying to establish Titan in Europe!

One of the memorable branding decisions Titan took in Europe was to have the brand name in beautiful, incandescent lighting displayed across the prestigious and popular Place de l'Opera in Paris. It was visible from all corners of the square, and even from a distance. However, the biggest hurdle they faced was breaking into the distribution network. As it turned out, the expected synergy between watches and jewellery export did not pay off. The watch sections were already full of brands and Titan found itself reeling to displace an existing brand. In order to secure distribution, it was necessary to make extravagant media commitments. Also, no major chain was prepared to try out Titan by the time the advertising campaign broke. While Titan, Vasant says, had appointed distributors all over Europe and had gained entry into a number of independent jewellery stores that also retailed watches, not many customers who walked in bought a Titan.

Even as the manufacturing facilities were being set up in India, Titan created a complex corporate structure for European operations centred around Dutch investment companies which would retain the profits they hoped to make in the European operations. 'The international holding structure – with the intellectual property rights of the brand being held by a Dutch company and operating companies in various geographies under a holding company – was a standard international structure, set up as guided by our tax consultant Arthur Anderson, for the purpose of tax planning. It did also "insulate" the Indian company from the international operations to some extent, as the overseas company affairs were reported separately [even though it was mentioned] in the annual report,' explains Vasant.

Xerxes's decision to introduce the India line in Europe didn't quite work as it was totally out of sync with European tastes, recalls Vasant. The lower end of the market was dominated by local brands, the middle by the Japanese while the upper end belonged to the Swiss brands, none of which made life any easier for Titan. So, after some small success initially, things didn't go as planned and business didn't pick up. 'Most people in the company were not behind it because it was a vision that they couldn't really think of and Xerxes's vision was 20 years ahead of its time,' says Vasant. Quality and delivery issues also began to plague the operation. Used to working in a monopolistic environment in India, Titan was unable to match up to the exacting standards of delivery and quality that watch retailing in Europe involved.

It was a struggle, recalls Ajoy Chawla, a young manager in the early 1990s who would later head new business incubation and strategy for Titan Company Ltd, even to pay salaries and the rent for the premises Titan had taken from Tata Ltd. The office secretary, Ajoy recalls, would keep reminding him in the last week of every month that salaries had to be paid. 'I would go around to the bank and find only some 500 to 600 pounds (approximately ₹28,000) in the account and then I would start chasing up on our collections from dealers. I would push for VAT refunds to get back duty paid for goods not sold. One of the small dealers had not paid up, so we went to court and got his car impounded. The court had his Mercedes sold and we got some 500 pounds for it. We used to generate cash through all kinds of legal, yet unconventional methods, besides regular ones like loans from Tata international subsidiaries!' says Ajoy.

Titan was selling unbranded jewellery in small quantities in Europe then and didn't need a warehouse, recalls Ajoy. So, they had a locker arrangement with the Royal Bank of Scotland; into that locker Ajoy and his small team would cram boxes of jewellery. Against orders by fax, Ajoy would personally pack and invoice the jewellery and then run to Royal Post to dispatch the packages to different parts of the UK.

It was the same with watches. They would come in cartons to a small warehouse in the basement of the London office where Ajoy and his team would sit on the floor and change the straps on them. 'I would suddenly get a call from the secretary to come urgently to the office for a business meeting. So, I used to freshen up and get to the office all suited and booted and the next minute I would be talking business plans for our European operations. It felt a bit weird as just a few minutes ago I was in the warehouse opening cartons and changing watch straps!' Ajoy returned to Indian operations in 1995 after spending a couple of years in the UK.

At the Basel fair, a must-go-to destination for watchmakers, Titan was given, along with the Chinese, space in an annexe away from the main halls, which were reserved for the Swiss. Shridhar Subramaniam, who was in the marketing team then and now heads Sony Music, recalls that you couldn't simply walk into any one of the Swiss stalls; you had to have an appointment. Anybody could enter as a visitor and look at what was showcased in the outside windows of the booths. But the booths themselves were out of bounds as they showcased new models the Swiss watchmakers did not want copied. So it was mostly press and dealers, no 'strangers'; it had nothing to do with an individual's nationality. 'Of course, they did entertain walk-ins if they felt they were potential customers, but sometimes charlatans did get in,' says Vasant.

It took something like guerrilla warfare to take on the Swiss monopoly. Acting on a brainwave, Xerxes's team prominently displayed their banners and brochures at a highly visible restaurant just outside the entrance to the main hall. 'All hell broke loose; the Swiss threw the book at us, saying it is illegal, and locked our booth. They had no legal basis for this and were using their influence to flex their muscles. We had to give in, remove our marketing materials, and only then did they allow us back in,' said Xerxes, guffawing at the memory.

Titan's woes in Europe, with the Swiss particularly, continued. When Titan tried to go the route of retailing through independent retailers, Swiss watchmakers told them that if they stocked Titan they wouldn't supply the Swiss brands. Titan had problems with distributors and employees, some of whom it found to be untrustworthy. Advertising money too was hard to come by. It had trouble with its designers, one of whom went to court saying Titan had sold many more watches than it had. Xerxes denied this charge outright.

For decades, European designs had been ornate, and Titan followed that trend. 'In the early 1990s, just before we entered the market, the trend moved entirely; [usually] at the Basel fair we couldn't find one square or rectangular watch. Suddenly, in the year of our launch, 1995, a new minimalism took over and our economics were in trouble. Ornate watches gave away to simple squares, rectangles, clean dials with very little ornamentation, no jewels encrusted, and we had to change our strategy all over again,' said Xerxes.

Titan had been an overnight success in India. It was not surprising, then, that it began to get impatient with what seemed likely to be a long slog in Europe. There was pressure from the board and it didn't seem like any easy shortcuts were available.

Against the advice of Jacques Mayer and senior executives who counselled that Titan didn't have the distribution yet to do a big burst of advertising, Xerxes had rolled the dice and spent a large sum of money on a pan-European advertising campaign. Unfortunately, the voices of caution were proven right and the returns from watches sold were much lower than expected. In a bid to cut losses, the team was pared and Vasant was recalled to India in 1998 to focus on Tanishq, another problem child at the time. David Saldhana, who had launched Tanishq in India was in turn sent to replace Vasant. (*The story of Titan's jewellery brand Tanishq and its launch is told in Chapter* 7.)

Stuck in the quagmire of Europe around the time of Xerxes's retirement in 2002, Titan had two things to celebrate. Its sales in the West Asia and Asia-Pacific region were fairly good. The West Asia operations were spearheaded by S. Ravi Kant (or SRK as he's known in Titan circles to distinguish him from Ravi Kant, the vice president of marketing and sales). SRK, who would later head Titan's watch business, had joined the company in the late 1980s. He had done a long stint in Dubai, heading the international subsidiary, responsible for marketing watches and jewellery in West Asia and Africa. He went through several interesting experiences of launching the brand in over 15 countries in this region, each of them having its own distinct flavour. One of the many high points of his stint there, SRK recalls, was selling customized Titan Edge watches in 'white gold' to the Emir of Qatar who loved gifting watches to the hundreds of people he met in his country or abroad.

Even in the highly-cluttered West Asian markets, Titan, SRK says, was among the first to launch 'branded' plain gold jewellery in Dubai. 'We were told by all the "experts" that in this market, where jewellery is displayed [and sold] like onions and potatoes at extremely competitive prices, you will never be able to command a premium for plain gold jewellery,' he says. It required many 'firsts' like these to establish Titan among the top three watch brands in many West Asian markets. Titan even created and launched a fragrance branded 'Evolve' during those early years. Evolve was created in France and promoted as a 'French' fragrance in order to stand its ground against other international brands.

In 1994, Raghu Menon was picked to head the Asia-Pacific subsidiary headquartered in Singapore, while Meera Harish was to head marketing for the region. Raghu had earlier been general manager, sales, then quit Titan for a few years, only to return as vice president. Raghu and Meera began with the proverbial low-hanging fruit and in quick succession, launched the brand in all the South Asian countries – Sri Lanka, Bangladesh, Nepal, Maldives, Myanmar and Bhutan. In fact, the recommendation for Titan's business partner in Bangladesh had come from none other than Simone Tata, chairperson of Lakmé. Pakistan was the only South Asian country that Titan could not launch in due to trade barriers.

It was an encore of the India success story as Titan established itself in all these markets. However, South-East Asia proved a hard nut to crack. The Asian financial crisis of 1997–98 had hit the countries in that region hard and all the economies were on a downward spiral. But the Titan team persisted. The initial years in Singapore were difficult. 'Watch retailers on Orchard Road, Singapore's top destination for shopping, would not even entertain a conversation with us; "Made in India" was not desirable,' says Meera. Titan was also launched in Malaysia, Thailand, the Philippines, Brunei, Vietnam, Indonesia, Australia, New Zealand and Fiji.

It took about five to six years of relentless marketing to get retailers in Singapore interested in Titan. When it did happen, the very same people who at one time wouldn't even entertain a conversation with Titan, the company, now invited the Titan team to coffee and lunch to discuss business strategy! For its part, Titan brought batches of retailers over to India to marvel at their factory. 'The Indian software industry had meanwhile been creating ripples globally and thus "Made in India" was becoming less of an impediment!' recalls Meera. It was a remarkable transformation in just a decade.

Xerxes was keen to break into Australia as well. As he loved to put it, 'An English-speaking, westernized, developed country located near Asia!' This happened in 1998, to much fanfare in the trade and the media. Meera was designated country manager, Australia and the South Pacific, and was posted in Sydney to set up and oversee operations. The consumer profile was similar to that obtained in the UK and Europe and so were the challenges: Indian brands were not exactly a selling proposition and Titan's core collection did not perform well. Fortunately, Meera hit a sweet spot when she recognized the potential of Australia's diverse population. The Greeks, Turks and Lebanese domiciled there loved Titan's solid gold watches, their prices ranging between A$1,000 (₹26,000) and A$1,250 (₹32,500), and what was threatening to be a dismal foray ended up becoming a success story. Simultaneously, Titan started selling significant volumes of its 18-carat gold jewellery to large chain stores like David Jones and Myers. Titan's sales down under also gave a boost to the benefits from the Export Promotion Capital Goods (EPCG) scheme that Titan was still in need of. Essentially, the company had to show export earnings against which it could import capital equipment for its watch and jewellery manufacturing, valued at several times the actual exports.

A few years later, when Tanishq started doing well in India, Titan decided to wind down its operations in Australia. In 2001, on her return from Sydney, Meera was made head of the Titan Asia-Pacific subsidiary. The director's report in the Annual Report for 2002-03, says it all: 'Titan International (Middle East), the associate company which looks after sales and marketing of its products in the Middle East and Africa, did well, selling over 3,00,000 watches. Sales turnover increased from $7.46 million (₹34.8 crore) to $7.87 million (₹37 crore), an increase of 5 per cent. Titan Watches & Jewellery International (Asia Pacific) Pte Ltd, the subsidiary company in Singapore, looking after sales and marketing in South Asia, South-East Asia, Australia and the South Pacific, had an exceptional year. While 2001–02 was the turnaround year for this company, 2002–03 was a year of growth. Sales turnover in 2002–03 grew by 28 per cent over the nine-month period ended 31 March 2002, going up from SGD 7.07 million (₹18.9 crore) to SGD 9.04 million (₹24.1 crore). This company wiped out its accumulated losses of the past.'

'However, Titan International Marketing Ltd, the associate company in London, continued to face difficult times. Its efforts to restrict operations to a few key markets with a view to contain costs saw sales volumes and values dropping significantly. Sales turnover fell from £3.44 million (₹26 crore) to £1.58 million (₹12 crore) and the net loss went up from £1.09 million (₹8.2 crore) to £1.24 million (₹9.4 crore). While a number of initiatives have been taken to cut costs even further, Europe remains the company's most difficult overseas market.'

As the report had observed, the picture in Europe was gloomy. Losses over the years aggregated about $14.5 million (₹68.4 crore) while Titan had invested $38.5 million (₹181 crore) in the European operations till then. Titan had managed to achieve its target of selling a lakh watches in the first year but could not ramp up subsequently and fell far short of its target of one million watches in seven years. The maximum it sold in any one year in Europe was around two lakh units. When David Saldanha, head of Titan Europe, came down to Bangalore for the annual business planning exercise for international markets, Xerxes welcomed him saying, 'Welcome, English patient!', clearly alluding, in jest of course, to the situation in his market. (*The English Patient* was an award-winning movie released that year.)

The poor showing of the European operations hit Titan's profitability at home. From profits after taxes of ₹25.09 crore in 1994–95, they steadily declined, punctuated only by the occasional good year, to ₹6.21 crore in 2002–03. It was a trying time for Bhaskar Bhat who took over as managing director in 2002. 'The big lesson we learned was that we needed to do pilots before any big launch. We went to 11 countries simultaneously and we took a big risk there. It was a good ambition to have but it was perhaps a little too early for us to dream so big; it could have been a more calibrated effort,' says Bhaskar, who decided to stop the European operations once he took over.

The management was asked to come up with a winding-up plan and bring back whatever cash remained and the stock. 'It was a difficult period: the audit committee had TIDCO representatives and there was a great deal of mistrust and suspicion. Their argument was that if this had happened in a government-owned company, the reaction would have been stronger. Thankfully, the Tata board stuck together and said that going to Europe was a joint decision and no one person could be held responsible,' says Bhaskar. Finally in 2004, a couple of years after Xerxes had retired, the European operations were brought to a stop. 'It was sad because it was Xerxes's dream. Perhaps we were too early,' explains Bhaskar.

The accumulated losses added up to ₹182 crore and it took several years for Titan to wipe it off the balance sheet. While Indian operations continued to be profitable – Titan made ₹25 crore in net profits in 2004–05 and ₹94.13 crore in 2006–07 – the overhang of the European losses bedevilled the company for a long time. The birth of Uttarakhand in the year 2000 as the 27th state of India was a godsend for Titan. The state government declared in 2003 that manufacturing in the state would attract no excise duties for 10 years and profits from a particular unit would attract no income tax for a certain period. That gave Titan substantial tax benefits as it was already assembling watches in the state, in Dehradun. With the excise and income tax waiver, higher profits could accrue to Titan. It set up two more watch-making units in Roorkee and Pant Nagar in the state to take advantage of this benefit and started producing more watches from these units. This gave a huge boost in writing down its losses, recalls Bhaskar. Titan followed its principle of community connect in Uttarakhand as it did in Tamil Nadu by recruiting young people, especially girls from the hills, as well as launching a significant CSR initiative in the state with Tata Trusts. Today, between the watches and jewellery plants in Uttarakhand, the company employs scores of people from the state.

Although TCS and Tata Unisys Ltd had an international presence, Titan's dream of building a global consumer brand was far ahead of its time. Even Infosys and Wipro were then just babes in the international woods. Subsequent efforts to acquire international brands and companies for the Tatas were anchored by Ishaat Hussain, a long-time Titan director. The Titan playbook was in a sense the forerunner for acquisitions by the Tata Group of Tetley, JLR (Jaguar Land Rover) and Corus, amongst other companies. Now after Europe, another challenge awaited Titan in the Indian market.

SIX

THE TIMEX AFFAIR

Europe wasn't the only dream that Titan was chasing. Sometime in early 1990, Titan's technical adviser Claude Gaudot and then executive vice president, Anil Manchanda, were in Delhi to meet with the Directorate General of Technical Development (DGTD). As the plane readied to land at Delhi airport, Claude suggested that Anil join him for drinks and dinner with Lawson Campbell, a former colleague at Timex, the US maker of wristwatches, famous for its oft-repeated slogan, 'takes a lickin' but keeps on tickin'.'

At the time, Lawson was acting chief executive of Timex India. Timex, the lowest cost producer of watches, chiefly plastic ones known for their reliability, had just set up a joint venture with Jayna Time Industries, a mid-level Delhi-based watchmaker. Since Anil had nothing better to do that evening, he said yes. 'I will never know if what followed was pre-planned by Lawson and Claude. We met at a palatial farmhouse on the outskirts of Delhi where Campbell stayed. In the course of the evening we were joined by Bob Werner, the visiting senior Timex executive responsible for India. Over convivial drinks and dinner, served by liveried waiters, we discussed sundry things including the political situation in India and USA, the economic outlook and the watch industry in India. Towards the end of dinner, Bob asked me if I would like to join Timex as their India head,' recalls Anil. This took Anil totally by surprise and he immediately told Bob that it was out of the question. Bob, however, insisted that Anil think it over and meet up for dinner the following day.

'I was already thinking in terms of a possible link-up between Timex and Titan, and I agreed. That night I spoke to Xerxes and he agreed that it was an idea worth pursuing. And so it came to pass that after dinner the following day I floated the possibility of a joint venture as the two companies had complementary skills,' says Anil.

Bob spoke to the chief executive officer of Timex, Jim Binns, who gave the green signal. The first thing Anil clarified was that there was no room for a third partner in the venture. Timex promptly agreed to buy off its existing partner. Then followed months of, sometimes difficult, negotiations in Bangalore, Bombay, Delhi, Hong Kong and Middlebury, Connecticut, where Timex is headquartered. By the time they signed a joint-venture agreement in June 1990, the negotiations had taken Titan-Timex almost six months. The venture was to make 2.5 million quartz watches a year. Timex would nominate the chairman, and Tata the chief executive who would handle day-to-day affairs. Meanwhile, Titan started working on a suitable name for the company and its products. The government's industrial policy dictated, rather inexplicably, that 'foreign brand names will not be permitted' and this clause had been included in the approvals given to Timex. Fortunately, this clause was dropped just before the joint venture filed for the initial public offer and cleared the path to calling the company Timex Watches Ltd.

Meanwhile, the TAS Secretariat at Bombay House, which handled the placements of the TAS officers and monitored their careers, suggested a potential candidate for the position of chief executive officer. Richard 'Dick' Masilamani joined Timex in 1991 after a four-year stint in a PepsiCo joint venture, representing the Tata Group through Voltas, which was a partner in the JV set-up between 1986 and 1987. He had earlier worked for TELCO (now Tata Motors) and then with Voltas till 1990 when Tata left the PepsiCo venture. Unfortunately, before Dick could join, trouble began to brew between the executives of Timex and Titan. Titan's technical team landed up in Noida, near Delhi, where the Timex office and factory were established, without prior intimation, and started throwing their weight around, recalls Anil. This lead to a huge fracas with the Timex team and a resolution meeting had to be set up in Hong Kong to pacify executives of both the companies. It was agreed that the Tatas would expedite the appointment of a CEO who would handle relationships, among other things, and in the meantime Titan's technical team was not to descend on Noida without prior arrangement.

Titan also worked out another agreement with Timex: Titan would move out of plastic watches – it was then manufacturing the Aqura brand – and focus on the higher end of the market with steel and other metals, while Timex would confine itself to plastic and the lower end of the market. Timex would also ride on Titan's marketing and distribution network, delivering economies of scale to both companies. 'We made an important sacrifice by handing over our successful Aqura brand (*see Chapter 8 for more on Aqura*) for which some in my team never forgave me,' recalled Xerxes. In fact, remembers Anil, 'we had to more or less come to a standstill with Aqura. Pricing power had peaked in the absence of access to special function movements while costs were rising apace as we were using regular all-metal movements for plastic watches.' Later, however, Xerxes had to relent to save the joint venture and Timex began to make metal watches as well.

Initially, Timex Watches Ltd launched 900 product offerings or stock keeping units (SKUs) to support a volume of two million watches a year. However, at the suggestion of Timex US, Timex India progressively reduced its offerings to 600 SKUs. 'Since the plastic watch market was not of a size that could support our capacity and targeted output of 2 million watches per year, we were subsequently allowed to design, produce and sell metal offerings,' says Dick.

Initially at launch there was 100 per cent complementarity because Timex was confined to plastics and Titan to metal. Timex offerings were priced in the ₹400–₹700 range while Titan was ₹700 plus a piece. Moreover, Titan was positioned as a fashion accessory while Timex projected itself as a wrist instrument that exploited digital technology and focused on outdoor and lifestyle activities. Some of the upper-end Timex watches gave blood pressure and pulse readings, and functioned underwater as well, apart from providing performance feedback to sportspersons during training and competitive events.

The billionaire chairman of the Timex group, Fred Olsen, on a visit to India, once asked Dick two questions. The first was: 'Do you know how many villages there are in your country?' Around 6,50,000, Dick replied. Olsen then asked his second question: 'If in each one of these a housewife or entrepreneur were to open a little watch shop in her/his house and sell just two watches a year, how much would this amount to?' Dick's answer was: 1.3 million a year. 'Here's your chance to capitalize on your rural market,' Olsen declared.

'Based on this we did a trial run by sending a special bus loaded with our products and entertainment material, including a video of the all-time hit movie *Sholay*. Our sales staff went to 25 villages in 10 days and did a lot of promo work and made attractive sales offerings. We spent ₹12 lakh on the project. While reports were aplenty that the rural people loved the razzmatazz, guess how many watches were sold? A grand total of two! This information was conveyed to our chairman, and was a good lesson for us in understanding India's rural markets!' says Dick.

The first annual general meeting of the company was a stormy one. Although Xerxes had pointed out that the company should not have its registered office in Delhi as the attending shareholders sometimes turned out to be unruly, nothing could be done about it as it had already been registered there. Predictably, at the very first meeting after going public, a bunch of shareholders complained about the food and demanded they be given watches as compensation. When Binns refused to relent, 'they started throwing things at us and we had to adjourn the meeting', said Xerxes chortling.

Perhaps these incidents were outward signs of the deteriorating relationship between Timex and Titan. Timex is a cost-conscious organization and was at that time the most economical producer of watches and also known for Indiglo, a hugely successful brand of luminescent watches that glowed in the dark at the press of a button. 'Titan on the other hand, was among the most expensive makers of watches. Our product design and development team, headed by Xerxes himself, rejected almost the entire Timex offering and started redesigning Timex products for the Indian market. In the process, the Timex watches became more and more like Titan's offering in both looks and costs, and the entire raison d'être of the joint venture was lost. Eventually, without a distinguishing product line and selling proposition there was no real reason for anyone to buy a Timex instead of a Titan,' recalls Anil.

In Dick's opinion, the Titan-Timex partnership broke down mainly for two reasons. On the one hand, Titan began to view Timex Watches Ltd as a threat to its share of the Indian watch market. On the other, Timex US was not willing – and to some extent was unable – to make the Indian joint venture a global manufacturing base. It was also reluctant to source from India, even though Timex India had emerged as a low-cost watch producer. 'There was a great opportunity for Titan and Timex to grow the Indian watch market by jointly promoting multi-watch ownership. I feel that if this had been taken seriously not only would the marketing costs for both companies have been lower and more effective, we could have expanded the Indian organized watch market and grown organically to mutual benefit,' says Dick.

By then it was too late; the relationship reached an impasse and then began a long battle to sell Titan's holdings in the company and arrive at a fair valuation. 'We had massive arguments, messages flew back and forth. I went to London for a final round of meetings with Michael Jacobi who had taken over from Jim Binns as president of Timex, and we finally settled on a pretty decent price and then pulled out by the late 1990s,' said Xerxes.

The relationship lasted for five years and Xerxes said it was a good experience as it helped expand the market for watches. The souring of the relationship with Timex was similar to the France Ebauches experience. As Anil recalls, by the time the phased localization of parts manufacture could be completed, Xerxes and François Perret were not on speaking terms owing to differences of opinion; all non-technical communication happened through Gaudot. They say that after the storm comes the calm, and so it was with the end of Titan-Timex. Titan launched a lower priced brand called Sonata in 1997. It came without the Titan label to fill the void created by Timex. Selling a shade over five million units a year, it is now a ₹528-crore brand in Titan's portfolio and is India's largest selling watch brand in numbers.

Titan's fortunes have come full circle in other ways too. In November 2011, it acquired the 280-year-old Favre Leuba, a household name in India in the 1960s and 1970s, for €2 million (₹13.8 crore). Exactly five years after it acquired the iconic but dormant Swiss brand, Titan Company Ltd relaunched it with

21 watches, all mechanical, and priced in the premium range of ₹1,18,000 to ₹3,82,000. The brand was the second oldest in the world, founded two years after another Swiss brand, Vacheron Constantin, which had been launched in 1735. The watches continue to be made in Switzerland and Titan has plans to invest a substantial sum in the company over a five-year period. Perhaps there is hope yet of Titan's European dream coming true.

SEVEN

TANISHQ BECOMES A BLOCKBUSTER

P. Latha remembers vividly the opening of the first Tanishq store in Chennai in July 1996. The store, of which she was the manager, on Cathedral Road, just off the landmark Gemini Circle, was like an art gallery with mood windows, suffused lighting, and done up in granite and green marble with low counters. There was little jewellery displayed compared to the traditional stores. It retailed diamond and gemstones-studded jewellery, all in 18-carat gold. The showroom had two sit-down counters for customers to browse at leisure; on the first floor, up the flight of stairs, was a lounge, a private viewing space, for the elite to shop in privacy.

The idea to enter into jewellery first took seed when, in 1990, Xerxes and Jayanti Prasad, Titan's public relations head, out of curiosity, dropped in at a jewellery exhibition held at the Taj Mahal Palace hotel, Mumbai, organized by the Gems and Jewellery Export Promotion Council. As they went around, Xerxes noted that most of the designs were mediocre and the workmanship quite ordinary. Jayanti and Xerxes talked about the shoddy way in which jewellers did business and how one could never be sure of the purity of the gold. This solidified a thought that had been forming in Xerxes's mind for a few years and he ventured, 'Why should the Tatas and Titan not take up jewellery manufacturing?' Although Anil Manchanda didn't exactly warm to the idea, he said, 'Let's explore it.'

At this time, Titan desperately needed to generate foreign currency in order to fund the purchase of the many imported components it needed to make watches. The year was 1991 and the country faced a critical situation with its foreign currency reserves depleted. Indeed, foreign exchange reserves had plunged so much that the country could finance only about 15 days worth of imports. According to a report in the *Indian Express*, the situation was so dire that in July 1991 the Reserve Bank of India had pledged 47 tonnes of gold with the Bank of England to raise a loan of $405 million (₹919 crore) and tide over a balance of payments crisis.

The P.V. Narasimha Rao-led government said that companies such as Titan would need to generate their own foreign exchange to fund their imports. 'We were told that the Government of India has no foreign currency to give you and you have to earn your foreign currency, so we started looking for a project that could make products we could sell and earn this forex; something we could sell overseas,' said Xerxes.

The search for products that would sell and simultaneously earn forex led to jewellery, a spark which was lit when Xerxes chanced upon the exhibition in Mumbai. Further, it seemed as though jewellery was a natural extension of watches as a fashion accessory: after all, both watches and jewellery were showcased at Basel, Switzerland. Indeed, the fair was called The World Watch & Jewellery Show!

Anil was put in charge of this project, despite his initial reservations. 'I came around to the view that if it was happening we could at least give a fair deal to the buyer,' he says. Shantharam, who was project manager for the watch plant earlier, was vested with the task of setting up the jewellery plant. Titan itself had no jewellery making expertise, but it so happened that the UK government had a programme for Commonwealth nations on the jewel trade. Under this programme, two technical consultants from the jewellery industry in the UK, Norman Walker and Mark Grant, were called in. These consultants were not in favour of a large plant as they were clear that the Indian market had nothing in common with the European or American markets; their advice was that Titan should proceed slowly. They also proposed that to begin with, Titan should set up a pilot plant and first test the less sophisticated end of the market.

Xerxes, however, overruled this suggestion and decided that Titan would go full steam ahead. So, a big jewellery plant was set up at Hosur with an investment of ₹65 crore in March 1993. As the project was meant to be a foreign-currency earner and Titan had decided to focus on exports to the European market to earn its foreign currency, a design office was set up in Paris at considerable cost. The designs were meant to be Western and European in their appeal. However, the project had a long gestation period and Titan would be ready to launch its jewellery in the European market only in 1995. In the meantime, the Indian economy had witnessed dramatic changes. Then finance minister Manmohan Singh's liberalization thrust from 1991 and the opening up of the economy had begun to see export earnings go up. As India's fledgling IT industry began to rake in the dollars, foreign currency was no longer an issue. Globally, too, things had begun to shift. 'By the mid-1990s there was a global downturn and an era of opulence had given way to austerity and minimalism and we found that it was turning out to be a mug's game,' said Xerxes.

Titan's blueprint at that stage was based on borrowings with no infusion of equity. Titan had one rights issue in 1992 but thereafter everything it did for several years was on borrowings, as its partner, TIDCO, said it had neither the money nor the inclination to dilute its stake. That prevented the Tatas from bringing in more equity. With many plans on the anvil, such as the European watch operations, a tie-up with Timex to market lower-end watches and a step-motor (a device which uses divider circuitry to reduce the frequency of the quartz crystal to a binary 0 or 1) plant, everything hinged on borrowings and debt. And here was Titan with a large and expensive jewellery plant and no overseas market to develop. Titan also spent a lot on design and packaging for the American market but didn't really make a dent in the market and had no fruitful outcome.

It was at this stage that it was decided that the company should focus on launching jewellery in the Indian market rather than a foreign one. On paper it looked promising given a huge but fragmented market comprising thousands of family jewellers. An informal survey had revealed that the downside was that business practices were vested with families and craftspersons. However, they believed that the Tata name could bring its weighty reputation for trust and fairness as it was an open secret that customers seldom really got all the gold they paid for; 'undercaratage' was rampant.

In jewellery parlance, 22-carat gold, or gold containing 91.6 per cent gold and 8.4 per cent alloys, was the preferred and de facto standard for Indian jewellery. However, in the absence of hallmarking or similar protection, many jewellers defrauded customers by palming off gold of lower purity, while selling it as 22 carat.'We were up against a mindset that believed implicitly in the family jeweller. One didn't go window-shopping for jewellery, you went to the family jeweller and he made jewellery for you. There were no jewellers who sold jewels made by others, we didn't have the skills to produce Indian jewellery and gem-set products. We had to turn to craftsmen spread across the country,' explained Xerxes.

For Titan too it was a learning experience, says Shantharam. *Karigars* or craftspersons and their families were brought from Kolkata, Mumbai and Delhi to Hosur. Titan's executives had to get the hang of how to buy gold as well as the stones and diamonds they would use to set in the gold. The consultants, Grant and Walker, also helped bring in expert stone-setters, master-makers, enamellers and other key craftspersons from various parts of Europe. They stayed for a couple of months to train the trainers. 'So the trainers were first trained and by that time I had recruited some people from the watches division, especially those who had an inclination for making jewellery,' explains Shantharam.

It was during Shantharam's time that a strong foundation was laid for technology transfer from a Swiss company for the refining and alloying of gold and a systematic training of new recruits and retraining of the *karigars* through experts from the Developing Countries Trade Association in master-making, casting, bench working, stone setting, polishing and enamelling.

The training was carried out in a structured manner. 'We asked them to do filing, fitting, drilling and sawing exercises. We trained them in drilling small holes. Initially, they used semi-precious stones, followed by CZ (cubic zirconia) diamonds; then they graduated to silver, then to gold. So, gold was not given from day one. They first had to demonstrate their skills. Similarly, there are different types of stone-setting from claw to channel setting. These exercises were taught first using semi-precious stones, then artificial and precious stones and finally diamonds,' explains Shantharam. Emphasis was also laid on mass manufacturing, controlling loss of gold in the process of making jewellery, creating a huge variety of jewellery, shortening delivery time as well as acquiring skills in the cost-efficient buying of gold and precious stones.

Despite his earlier reservations, J.R.D. was excited about the project, as was Tata Sons' director, Jamshed Bhabha. Harish Bhat, who worked for several years in Titan both in the watches and jewellery business, and is now brand custodian for Tata Sons, recounts in his book, *Tata Log*, 'Jamshed Bhabha was vocal in his support for the jewellery business. He proudly showed Xerxes a picture of his aunt, Lady Meherbai Tata, wife of Sir Dorab Tata, standing next to Queen Mary and wearing the monumental Jubilee diamond that weighed an amazing 245 carats (49.07 g). It was sold by the Tata family in the 1930s to Cartier, then to jeweller Harry Winston, who sold it to a French billionaire, who in turn sold it to diamond czar Robert Mouawad, the current owner of the gem.' The history of association with jewels within the Tata family contributed to this support.

However, not all directors were gung-ho about the idea. Ishaat Hussain, former finance director of Tata Sons, who served on Titan's board for almost 27 years, was one of the sceptics. 'My reservation about jewellery was that I didn't know if the business model lent itself to scale, corporate management and factory manufacture. Jewellery trade at that time was dominated by families, small in scale, and jewels were all handmade. And the jewellery people wore in the north was very different from [what was worn in] the south,' explains Ishaat as we chat in his office in Mumbai.

In any case, having decided to launch in the Indian market, Titan needed to come up with a good brand name. 'Titan Jewellery' didn't have the right ring to it. Names such as Aurum, the Latin word for gold, were bandied about, but Xerxes was of the opinion that it would not appeal to domestic customers. 'Celeste' was a brand name Titan used in Europe but it had already been registered in India by another company. In spite of many ideas going back and forth, nothing seemed to fit right; the only thing Xerxes was sure of was that it should have a feminine and Indian feel to it.

Meera Harish, who had moved from Titan's watch sales and marketing to jewellery as product manager in early 1994, was at this point vested with the task of putting together a shortlist of brand names. 'Mr Desai asked me to go and buy an eclectic collection of books to research possible brand names. I was excited! I went to Gangarams, the largest bookstore in Bangalore then, and also another lovely, cool bookstore, R&B, on Ulsoor Road and bought all kinds of coffee-table books on architecture, dance, and culture, pore over them and then go with a list of 10 or 15 suggestions to Mr Desai's office. He would shoot them all down and push me for more and tell me to find more inspiration,' she recalls. One day, a couple of weeks later, Meera had the word 'Nishka' on her list from a book she had picked up at R&B: it meant 'coin' in Hindi. Xerxes liked it. He wrestled with it, first knocking off the 'k' and making it Nishqa. 'I am fond of dogs, and I owned a Harlequin Great Dane at that time called Monishqa. Also, the young daughter of a close friend was called Monisha. That triggered Tanishq,' Xerxes recalled. Tanishq also reflected the promoters' names: Tata and Tamil Nadu. Sliced differently, it also meant 'Tan' (body) and 'Ishq' (love). More than anything, Xerxes loved the romance the word 'Tanishq' connoted. Meera recalls bumping into friends in Mumbai many years later: one of them had named her daughter Tanishq and told her there were quite a few others with that name – all inspired by the Tata jewellery brand.

Was it hubris that made the Titan team believe that having conquered a large chunk of the market for quartz watches, it could change mindsets in India regarding gold jewellery? Revathi Kant, who is now the chief design officer for Titan Company Ltd and was in charge of market research then, remembers suggesting carrying out market research to see how receptive people would be to buying 18-carat instead of 22-carat gold. In order to be successful, Titan was banking on a gigantic cultural shift in habits among Indian customers. In the end, though, no research was conducted and Titan plunged into making 18-carat jewellery. Xerxes and team were confident that they could transform the jewellery market in the same way they had transformed the watch market. Tanishq wanted to offer more studded jewellery than plain gold jewellery; gold prices were known to everybody and such jewellery offered little by way of differentiation. The margins for studded jewellery, the team thought, would also be better as customers could not accurately value gems. Besides, the Tanishq range would feature innovative designs.

When the upmarket Tanishq store opened on Cathedral Road, customers were curious but were intimidated by the fact that they had to fix an appointment with the store manager before visiting. All this was new to Chennai. 'We had very exclusive designs. I don't think the customers had seen such designs before. The designers, trained at the National Institute of Fashion Technology (NIFT), had done a good job. The [jewellery was] well received. There was also a buzz around the Tata Group having launched a jewellery brand. But the walk-ins were low,' recalls Latha.

Gold buyers wanted jewellery in 22-carat gold while Tanishq's offerings were in 18 carat which rendered the metal harder and therefore resistant to scratches and dents, apart from enabling the stones to be held with a firmer grip. However, 70 per cent of the customers in Chennai comprised buyers who preferred plain gold jewellery to gem-studded jewellery. Unsurprisingly, sales from this Tanishq store in the eight-month period up to March 1997 was only ₹2.8 crore, far below the target of ₹3.5 crore. Tanishq would have to do several course corrections before it could emerge as a blockbuster brand in the mid-2000s and establish Titan as a jewellery company.

Although 18-carat gold was the world standard for fine jewellery, a few markets such as India are exceptions to this rule. But, as with their watches, Titan wooed Indian consumers with international styles and designs. The stores gave the appearance of high-end international boutiques, upending the souk-like atmosphere of most Indian jewellery stores. But the marketing team overlooked one important point. Indian consumers bought jewellery not only for its own sake, but for the value of the gold. Titan's 1996–97 Annual Report acknowledges this fact:

> While Tanishq jewellery has drawn praise and evoked a very favourable reaction among consumers, the fact that our collection was initially confined to only 18-carat gold jewellery, mostly gem set, proved to be a limiting factor in the attainment of volume objectives. Work, therefore, commenced in right earnest on the creation of a new collection of 22-carat gold jewellery based on traditional Indian design themes.
>
> While the company believes that an 18-carat gold alloy is the most suited for jewellery – and is, in fact, the world standard for fine gold jewellery – the existence of a very strong consumer preference in India for 22-carat gold jewellery cannot be wished away. Our entry into this market segment will, it is hoped, accelerate the trend towards an official hallmarking process which will significantly benefit the consumer who, today, is often the recipient of substantially undercarataged jewellery masquerading under the 22-carat label.

From 1996, when Tanishq was launched, to the year 2000, Titan ran a tough course. The European operations were slowing down and bleeding the core watch business, which funded Titan's growth, and Tanishq wasn't going anywhere. Losses in the jewellery business in India alone totted up to ₹100 crore as sales refused to pick up. The mid-course correction that was planned – to change to Indian designs and refurbish the already established boutiques to suit local tastes – took time. As Titan's Managing Director Bhaskar Bhat recalls, Tanishq was deep in debt and there was speculation that the Tata Group would sell the jewellery business. 'The European-style jewellery we introduced in 18 carat was a disaster. The going was rough [through these years],' he says.

Vasant Nangia was put in charge of the struggling jewellery business and the launch of 22-carat jewellery in June 1997 did help. The Tanishq retail chain had 14 exclusive boutiques in 12 cities by then with a combined floor space of 31,000 square feet, making it India's first jewellery store chain. In 1997–98 sales rose to ₹52 crore as against ₹21 crore the previous year. But Vasant was horrified to find that the domestic jewellery business, which was about half of the total Tanishq business (the rest being international sales of jewellery), was making losses virtually equal to the turnover. The general mood was that the jewellery division should be sold, or at least spun off, so that it did not sink the whole ship.

Sensing this, Vasant recalls telling Xerxes, 'Let's face it. The watch industry in India has become an oligopoly of sorts, with major protection barriers. But the jewellery business is very different: we have competition in all shapes and forms, in every city and street. We've learnt in Europe what brutal competition can do. It's a gamble with Tanishq, but if we are to succeed, we need to build a completely different culture, different ways of management.'

Once Xerxes gave Vasant a free hand, he handpicked a team from the watch division, including Johnson Verghese, then head of the western region, and a bunch of bright youngsters from various functions. The team set to work revamping the business. 'We had to fix the basics. Jewellery buyers in India demand to know gold weight, diamond weight, making charges,' says Vasant. The pricing system was changed and the price tags now displayed gold and gem details that helped in-store staff explain the prices of each product better to customers. Store layouts were changed to cater to a larger product line. Even display trays, uniforms and training programmes were redesigned.

Another big move was to bring the product into sharper focus. A system of weekly selection meetings was introduced where product development teams would present prototypes of new designs. Each design was subjected to critical scrutiny to ensure value to customers. To take cognizance of differences in taste between one city and another, a quarterly buying meet (QBM) was put in place so that store managers and franchisees could see all the designs under one roof and choose what was suitable for their markets. This created a sense of ownership and proved to be a powerful way of engaging staff and franchisees.

But there was still something missing. How was the brand to win over Indian customers who had been closely tied to family jewellers for generations? The trick was to deal with the problem of undercaratage without having to melt and test the jewellery in a laboratory; it was important to find an easy way of demonstrating undercaratage.

Meanwhile, on a visit to the World Watch & Jewellery Show in Basel in 1996 Shantharam spotted an X-ray fluorescence machine that used spectroscopy to measure the purity or caratage of gold in less than three minutes. It used a non-destructive process and also showed the content and presence of the alloys in it.

Vasant and his team too immediately saw the hidden potential of this instrument. 'I went to Xerxes and said, look we have to prove to people what we are saying, that [they] are buying impure gold,' says Vasant. 'Hats off to him. He said, "I agree with you" and said go ahead and put it in the stores. We had14 then. At that time [the machines were] around ₹10 to ₹12 lakh each. It needed guts to make that decision, especially since Tanishq was not making money.' The obscure scientific instrument soon acquired a brand name – Karatmeter – thanks to inputs from Joseph George who had been assigned as the account manager for Tanishq from the advertising agency, Lintas.

But its effectiveness had to be tested and for this, the team chose a franchisee store in Indore. 'We wanted to test it in a high gold-consuming city where we knew that caratage issues would be high,' says Vasant. The morning of the test there was an ad in the newspaper saying, 'There's a thief in the family'; it then went on to talk about the family jeweller. It invited people to come to the store and test their gold for free. A few came in tentatively and were dismayed to find their jewellery was impure. Word began to spread and soon there were hundreds of people thronging to the store.

One woman who put a heavy bangle on the Karatmeter was shocked to find it was made of 11-carat gold. Many women started wailing upon discovering how impure their jewellery was. Soon, jewellers burst into the store shouting, '*Yeh kya kar rahe ho*, what are you doing, you are destroying our business!' What followed was mayhem and the police had to be called in to restore order.

Old-timers G. Rajendran and P. Sukumaran, who have been with Tanishq right from its inception, recall how they did road shows in the smaller towns of Tamil Nadu and Karnataka to promote the brand. They mounted exhibitions at local halls or hotels, put up posters, ran ads and, as in an election, sent autorickshaws fitted with loudspeakers to go around town announcing the exhibition. 'Now this was not the Titan way of doing business but at that time we didn't bother as we had to reach customers. That was our priority. It was necessary for our survival,' says Rajendran. During the road shows Tanishq kicked off an exchange-your-old-jewellery scheme and the jewellery was melted in front of customers. Many, says Rajendran, felt all this diluted Tanishq's image, but it's from these road shows that the idea emerged to launch Gold Plus, a brand of pure gold jewellery for the mid-level market and smaller towns.

Riding on the newfound credibility of Tanishq, Vasant's team simultaneously started approaching the institutional market for special and bulk orders. An order from carmaker Maruti Udyog Ltd for 50,000 inscribed gold coins as gifts for its dealers in 1997 on the occasion of its 15th anniversary, was the largest in the company's history. Vasant personally negotiated the order which went through a number of rounds of negotiation at various levels at Maruti's office in Delhi. 'We made these coins and delivered them even though we didn't even have a proper logistics system in place,' recalls Rajendran. Fulfilling this commitment was an eye-opener of sorts and a morale-booster, showing that Tanishq had the capability to execute bulk orders. 'It was the biggest single order for that time and challenging too in terms of tooling, gold procurement (all of 750 kg), a lead time of just two months and hand delivery to specific locations. It gave Tanishq an opportunity to test speed of response, improve procurement efficiency, tool design and fabrication skills, and improve distribution efficiency,' explains Shantharam. Tanishq did not receive a similar bulk order after that but as Vasant points out, it opened the door to smaller corporate orders and got the brand a lot of publicity.

It was April 2000 and Tanishq had launched its 36th showroom in Pune. Speaking to the *Times of India,* a triumphant Xerxes declared that the company's jewellery business had grown to ₹150 crore in 1999–2000, and had made a profit in the first quarter of that year. As that year's Annual Report observed:

> Shareholders will be pleased to know that the jewellery division started the current year on a happy note by registering a profit for the first quarter. Your directors believe that the jewellery business will provide valuable top line and bottom line support to your company even as the watch business enters more competitive times.

It was the beginning of Tanishq's ride to the top as Titan's blockbuster brand.

Gradually, the mood in Titan began to change. Vasant recalls, 'The jewellery division had always been the poor cousin of the watch division. Just a couple of years earlier, we used to be told, "Oh here are the guys who are bleeding the company dry. How long can we keep giving them handouts?" The same sceptics in the watch division now wanted to claim a share in the success.'

However, in May 2000, there was an unexpected development. Jacob Kurian, who then headed Titan's domestic watch marketing, remembers the day vividly. Titan had just been judged *Brand Equity*'s Brand of the Year and Vasant had been appointed as the chief operating officer of the company. When Jacob went to Vasant's room to congratulate him, Vasant asked Jacob to wait, saying he needed to meet Xerxes first. 'Vasant later walked into my room and as I got up to congratulate him, he said, "I've quit." I was shocked. No one in the company had any inkling of this,' says Jacob. It then came to light that along with a handful of Tanishq executives, who at this point quit en masse, Vasant planned to set up a fashion jewellery brand for youth, Oyzterbay. Stunned by the turn of events, Titan later engaged in a lengthy legal battle with Vasant for breach of contract; a battle Titan eventually lost.

That weekend, Jacob got a call from Xerxes to meet him at his house: he wanted Jacob to take charge of Tanishq. 'I said I'll think about it as I wasn't sure, but out of respect for Xerxes I had to come up with a credible reason to say no,' he recalls. Jacob used to pass by a traditional jeweller, Bhimas, on Dickenson Road in Bangalore, every day and always found it crowded but the Tanishq store nearby was invariably empty. 'So I went back to Xerxes and told him I'm taking it up for the sheer intellectual curiosity [as to] why a corporate can't succeed in this business. We had been six years in this business [at that time].'

Jacob then laid out his terms: everyone in Tanishq, from manufacturing and finance to human resources and marketing, had to report to him. 'I knew what the manufacturing guys were capable of as I had sold the jewellery they made; I had worked with them when I was selling in the international markets,' he says. Xerxes acquiesced. Shantharam chose to move out of Tanishq manufacturing, and was given the position of chief manufacturing officer (watches).

Meanwhile, Vasant's departure presented the press with grist for the mill and many predictions were made about Tanishq's imminent demise. Morale in the company was down and everyone felt besieged. In order to allay fears, franchisees from all over India were invited to the Taj West End where the entire management of Titan stood together to promise that the jewellery business had the unwavering support of the company and that they should not worry. 'Even though we broke even and we were feeling great about ourselves, there was still a great deal of hostility at the board level,' says Jacob. Luckily, the representatives of TIDCO on the board were very encouraging because they saw the potential of the jewellery business in India. 'In fact, they cited the example of the many booming jewellery stores in and around Chennai's Panagal Park [the city's gold district] to bolster the Tanishq cause,' says Jacob.

However, Bombay House was unhappy with the Tanishq business. Much acrimonious correspondence flew between Xerxes and Ishaat as well. Jacob recalls how Ratan Tata famously asked if Titan was a watch company with a jewellery business or a jewellery company with a watch business! In order to get a sense of the real picture, the board engaged management consultancy McKinsey to study and analyse the business verticals.

Jacob remembers McKinsey's Ireena Vittal (who, incidentally, is on the board of Titan now as an independent director) walking into his room one morning. 'I was ready to tell her all about the turnaround in the business, but her first question was: "So,

Jacob, tell me why we shouldn't shut down this business." I was surprised because I thought they were here to assess the business but it looked like they had been sent with the express intention of shutting it down.' Eight weeks later, though, McKinsey concluded that the business could be put on a sound footing. 'Tanishq was actually a very attractive bet for the company. But they had to think of themselves as a retailer. They hadn't done that till then; they saw themselves as a product company at that point of time. In watches, they had multiple channels to sell, whereas in Tanishq they were a retailer,' explains Ireena.

After the assessment by McKinsey, there was to be a presentation at Bombay House. It was the first presentation on Titan's businesses to the Tata Sons board after Bhaskar had taken over as managing director. When Jacob volunteered to make the first presentation on Tanishq, the latter had misgivings. He felt the board would see red upon hearing the word 'jewellery'. But Jacob insisted. 'You know the numbers are great now, so don't worry,' he told Bhaskar. Also present at the meeting were two McKinsey officials involved in the Tanishq study, Ranjit Pandit and Gautam Kumra. Following Jacob's passionate exposition to the board on the Tanishq business and its potential, only a deathly silence ensued. Unable to bear the tension, Gautam addressed himself directly to the chairman, Ratan Tata: 'So, Mr Tata what do you think of this business?' Tata's response, after a further studied silence, was that the business was doing reasonably well and the board should give it some more time. That was the endorsement the Tanishq team was looking for.

'Whatever fee we paid McKinsey was paid back to us in full by that one question Gautam asked Mr Tata, because none of us would have had the guts to ask it!' says Jacob laughing at the recollection. 'You see, as part of management, we were at the receiving end and McKinsey had more credibility, so they could counsel Mr Tata to give us one more chance,' recalls Bhaskar.

Gautam, who would go on to be the managing director of McKinsey India, chuckles when reminded of his 'momentous' question. He says the Tata brand always stood for trust and people were prepared to pay a premium for it. 'Tanishq was a niche player and we felt there was an opportunity for it to become mainstream as a [major part] of the jewellery buying happens around weddings,' he says.

The Tanishq team was bolstered with Harish Bhat joining Titan in 2001 as vice president. Harish moved to Titan from Tata Tea where he had led marketing of its tea brands. In March 2002, Harish attended the Tanishq business associates' meeting at the famed Taj Fort Aguada resort in Goa. Xerxes had been project manager for this hotel many years ago when it was being built. Jacob made an impassioned pitch, pacing up and down the stage, and spelt out the vision for Tanishq, saying it had had enough of having 'lived' off Titan's watch business for all these years. 'Everyone gave him a standing ovation for several minutes. It was very important when the business was going through a tough phase for the leader to inspire and galvanize the team for the future,' says Harish. Xerxes came to Fort Aguada at the end of this progamme as it was to be his farewell to the Tanishq team for he was retiring. Also present at the meeting was the famous Goa-based cartoonist Mario Miranda, a friend of Xerxes.

Jacob continued to have town hall meetings on the shop floor, one of the things he had learned from former Tata Steel chairman Russi Mody when the latter had given a lecture at the Xavier School of Management (XLRI) in Jamshedpur where Jacob had been a student. 'I even told them that we have one year to turn around the business or they and I will all be out of jobs. They were stunned as the factory staff had no idea how badly Tanishq was doing since they were getting the same wages and increments as the watch business staff,' says Jacob.

On the ground, however, nothing much changed. People still came into the stores to check their jewellery on the Karatmeter and went back to lambast their jewellers. Sales didn't pick up and the Tanishq team was at its wits' end. The advertising only served to reinforce the perception that it was a high-priced brand. Tanishq's early ads, one of which featured actor Malaika Arora, were presented in a Western ambience and showed only studded and diamond jewellery. All this served to reinforce the elitist profile that Tanishq had adopted for its stores as well.

Then, one day, the penny dropped. Jacob was at the Dickenson Road outlet when a lady walked in, tested her jewellery on the Karatmeter and made to leave, looking extremely flustered. Jacob intercepted her and asked if he could be of help. 'You don't do anything to solve our problem,' she snapped at him. 'All you do are things to make us feel bad!' Upon inquiry, the store staff told him the test had revealed that her jewellery was only 17 carats, not 22. Jacob ran this information and the customer's reaction over and over in his head. That's when it struck him: the Karatmeter was telling people their jewellery was worth a lot less than they thought and that they had been made fools of, but Tanishq was not offering a solution to the problem.

After some serious brainstorming, Tanishq came up with an idea that almost gave the finance head, Khushroo Kapadia, a heart attack, Jacob recalls chuckling. It would, in a sense, reverse matters for customers through the 'Impure to Pure' scheme. Tanishq offered to exchange old jewellery for new 22-carat ones. Harish Bhat explains that the scheme was called 19=22. Women could bring in their gold jewellery and test it on the Karatmeter. If the purity of their jewellery was lower than 22 carat and higher than 19 carat, it could be exchanged for Tanishq's 22-carat jewellery of their choice by paying only the manufacturing charges. Tanishq would bear the cost of the gold.

On the evening the scheme was launched, Jacob dispatched one of the staff to check out the stores. 'He called me from the Dickenson Road store and asked me to come immediately to see for myself. I thought it was another disaster in the making. When I asked what happened he said in great excitement: "There are people in our store!" We got into a car and went to the store. It was like a zoo!' recalls Jacob. The key had been to identify the problem and offer a solution. It was not surprising that this scheme became popular all over India.

Harish, who took over as chief operating officer, Tanishq, when Jacob quit in 2003, recalls the festival sale over Diwali that year, which was huge for the brand in terms of sales. 'We would be dialling stores around the country to tally the sales for the day and see if it had exceeded targets and go home after midnight, much after the last customers had left our stores,' he says. Several of Tanishq's stores registered sales of over ₹1 crore on that one day.

Other things were also tweaked at the factory end. In 2003, Jacob recruited L.R. Natarajan (LRN) to head manufacturing. LRN was from the automobile industry with no background in jewellery but was known for thinking out of the box. Under his watch, the Tanishq factory saw unparalleled change. What was required to transform the factory was not an incremental improvement, but a quantum leap in productivity, and he ensured that. From being oriented to large-scale batch manufacturing processes, the factory focus shifted to being more oriented towards bespoke jewellery. Today, the factory can churn out 30,000 unique pieces of jewellery a day; at one time it could hardly manage 200–300 pieces a month. Tanishq also started what it called *karigar* parks near the factory at Hosur; this brought under one roof goldsmiths and craftspersons from different regions, all working under better conditions in terms of lighting, seating, hostel accommodation and remuneration.

The 2002–03 Annual Report marks the transformation in the following way:

> The jewellery division once again turned in an impressive 29 per cent growth in operating income which increased from ₹267.66 crore to ₹345.03 crore. The division's profit before taxes grew by 129 per cent to ₹5.37 crore. The jewellery business provides much needed balance to the Company's fortunes as the watch business faces increasing competition in India.

This was a major change in fortunes from a time the business faced the threat of closure.

Meera, the head of marketing, category management and design, recalls the presentation she made to the board in early 2004. The title of the presentation, 'Dil Se', borrowed from film-maker Mani Ratnam's eponymous film, reflected the strategic marketing challenges for Tanishq as she spoke literally from the heart. According to her presentation, consumer research continued to show that awareness of 22-carat jewellery marketed by Tanishq was low, and that Tanishq was perceived to be more expensive than it actually was. Secondly, the question was how to make diamonds more accessible and affordable. In time, Meera's presentation led to the birth of Tanishq Daytimes – a diamond workwear collection that was launched with a lively television campaign. That was Tanishq's first year of creating a value perception campaign.

Das Narayandas, a professor at Harvard Business School, who is now on Titan's board of directors, wrote an extensive case study on Tanishq in 2006, titled 'Positioning to capture the Indian woman's heart'. In it he wrote about the several new collections that were launched by Tanishq that gave a big boost to its sales: 'Daytimes, a diamond-based collection, aimed to reposition diamonds as affordable, casual, young and contemporary; Aarka, a high-fashion 22-carat gold collection aimed to position Tanishq's design and image skills, was a joint initiative with fashion designer Sabyasachi Mukherjee; Aamra, a collection of studded jewellery, attempted to tackle Tanishq's forbidding image with a traditional studded collection inspired by a mango motif. Wedding and festival collections were also launched. The brand was associated with several high-profile fashion events to integrate product design and communication efforts, including designing the Femina Miss India beauty pageant crown, as well as participating in the Milan Fashion Week. The results were spectacular with sales well exceeding the ambitious target of ₹550 crore and closing out at ₹570 crore.'

The case study also highlights a one-year exercise that Tanishq completed in October 2005 on its brand value proposition. 'The latest iteration of the brand conception was complex – attempting to capture the contemporary Indian woman's careful negotiation of the traditional and modern. Tanishq had not positioned itself as a progressive Indian brand that combined tradition and heritage. *Paheli*, a major Bollywood fairytale, captured many of these themes, and Tanishq scored a coup by designing the jewellery for the film. A historical romance, the film replicated the authentic Rajasthan style and incorporated period pieces in the actors' clothing and jewellery. Tanishq carried these themes over into a series of TV ads echoing the *Paheli* theme. While the movie was not a hit, it was nominated for an Oscar; the Tanishq Paheli line, on the other hand, was a sell-out success.'

Tanishq's Bollywood associations would continue in the future as well. It would help the brand to gain a wider presence. In 2005, Harish moved to Tata Telecom for a year and returned to Titan in 2006 to head the watch business. C.K. Venkataraman, the present chief executive officer of Tanishq, took over from him. Venkat says the brand did many things over the past decade. He draws attention to the fact that the company has focused on several aspects of manufacture and operations. It has revitalized tradition by making jewellery designs more contemporary. Its advertising too had changed to reflect more of an Indian flavour and it showed the plain gold jewellery Tanishq had to offer. It introduced the hugely successful Golden Harvest instalment scheme to buy jewellery. It enabled customers to pay in instalments for 11 months and at the end of the 12th month they could buy jewellery at a Tanishq store with the company contributing to the 12th instalment. The scheme ensured a return of 16 per cent to the depositor on their investment. However, this scheme had to undergo a change in 2014 as the government defined such instalments and schemes as public deposits and put a ceiling on the rate of interest they could offer. The Golden Harvest now works exactly as it did earlier, the only difference being the rate of return which is now capped at 12 per cent. Tanishq also tied up a different funding method for gold procurement by taking it on lease from international banks and paying for it as and when the jewellery gets sold. This reduced Tanishq's working capital requirement and the need to invest and stock gold.

While the earlier stores were smaller in size, large Tanishq stores were opened stocking the entire range of jewellery. 'Now we have seven such stores and each one of them has redefined our stature in the city they are in and increased our share,' says Venkat. Approximately 8,000-square feet each, these stores are located in Mumbai, Pune, Delhi, Lucknow, Kolkata, Ahmedabad and Chennai. Typically, they stock at least 10,000 pieces of jewellery as compared to 6,000 pieces in the smaller stores.

Revathi Kant says the brand is also conscious of the regional influences in jewellery design. The other insight Tanishq unearthed in its research, she says, is the growing market for jewellery for working women. 'This market was non-existent, but today we have created this segment. The key takeaways from our research were that women wanted affordability and ease of wear. Traditional jewellery looked too ornate for the clothes women wore to work,' she explains. The discovery of the existence of this market segment led to a line called Mia, in 14-carat gold, thus making the entire collection more affordable at prices starting from ₹3,999. Tanishq also launched the upper-end Zoya collection with stores only in Mumbai and Delhi, to cater to a niche and exclusive customer segment. Zoya uses more precious metals in its jewellery and reflects a higher quality of workmanship, points out Revathi. Prices start at ₹70,000 for small items like finger rings and can go up to ₹70 lakh for more elaborate prices of jewellery.

The Tanishq factory had made impressive strides in its journey of innovation under LRN. After all, 'We shall challenge the obvious and the safe,' has been a key Tanishq tenet. LRN ensured, through a systematic, multi-pronged process-oriented approach, that 'the ability to think innovatively' had been infused into the minds of all employees at the factory. When Tanishq won the prestigious *Harvard Business Review*/McKinsey M-Prize, Jacob summed it up perfectly when he said to LRN that the fact that 'Tanishq's innovation journey was not dependent on a single Steve Jobs but was built in the minds and hearts of many individuals augurs well for the brand and the company'. (The M-prize is an open innovation project aimed at reinventing management for the 21st century.)

Tanishq is the clear market leader in many cities in India: Delhi NCR region, Chandigarh, Lucknow, Patna, Bhubaneshwar, Mumbai and Ahmedabad. In the southern cities, many strong local brands rule the roost, but none of them have the national footprint to match Tanishq. In the financial year 2017–18, Tanishq notched up sales of ₹13,036 crore, dwarfing the watch business which had revenues of ₹2,126 crore. Ratan Tata's comment, made somewhat ironically a decade earlier that Titan was a jewellery company with a watch business, finally came to be true.

After Ratan Tata demitted office as executive chairman of the Tata Group, he moved to the Tata Trusts office in the colonial-era

Elphinstone building in the Fort area of Mumbai. The office itself is minimalistic, with light streaming in from a balcony garden. Seated on a leather sofa, with the sunlight warming my back, I ask Mr Tata about his opposition to the jewellery business in the early days. In a measured voice, he explains, 'My recollection of that episode was that the board of Tata Sons was divided on what should be done. Xerxes's strongest supporter at that time was J.R.D. Tata. It was he who felt that this should happen, not for any well-defined reason other than that he believed in Xerxes's vision. So, he overruled the dissidents on the board and in a manner of speaking the board became very passive on this issue. I'm pleased that they had such success with the jewellery business.' And did he, I persist, at any time ask the company to go slow on the project? 'I didn't, but I was also one of the people who was not very excited about the jewellery business,' Tata replies in his gravelly voice.

Bhaskar recalls that after Tanishq became a success, Ratan Tata, at a business excellence committee meeting graciously acknowledged the success of Titan. 'I was there at that meeting as mentor for another company, not as part of Titan. He said, "We have been proved wrong".' Ishaat Hussain, who had opposed the jewellery business in the early days, acknowledges Xerxes's vision. 'I take my hat off to Xerxes who saw that he needed another growth engine because the watch business would only take Titan so far; he took that call and persevered with it,' he says.

In 2016, Titan invested in CaratLane, an online jewellery company, to tap into the increasing trend of digital shopping. The site offers fine jewellery in gold and diamonds for everyday wear. With 36 stores across the country, CaratLane also has a growing store presence, making it an omni-channel jewellery brand. It reported a turnover of ₹290 crore in 2017–18.

The jewellery business recorded its best-ever performance since inception in 2017–18. The total revenues rose by 20 per cent for the second consecutive year, outperforming both the national and local/regional competition. Once regarded as a gap in its business, Tanishq now garners a high share in the wedding jewellery segment as well as in the high-value diamond jewellery segment. With 45 new stores opening in the last year and a presence in 159 towns, Tanishq expects to sparkle brighter.

Farewell, Xerxes

By the time Xerxes Desai retired, he had built the 'Jewel in the Tata crown'. As the founding managing director of Titan Watches Ltd (now Titan Company Ltd), he had succeeded in creating an organization that came to be known for its innovative, bold and relaxed culture, one that attracted and nurtured the best talent and was a great place to work in. Xerxes was always fond of saying that a space of work should be a place of joy. His vision largely contributed to the company being recognized as one of the top consumer brands to have been created in India.

Xerxes's retirement in 2002 was a momentous occasion and the entire company and all its business associates across India prepared to give him a fitting send-off. In fact, there were so many farewell parties for Xerxes that for about a month or so, he attended them at the rate of one a day! Among those functions, there was one event at the Taj Residency in Bengaluru, one at the Hosur factory and one at the Golden Spa Resort in Peenya on the outskirts of the city, hosted by Titan's business associates, many of whose fortunes had been derived from the company that Xerxes had created. Many former employees flew in especially to participate in the ceremonies at various venues. At the Taj Residency in Bangalore, for instance, he was ushered into the hall to the strains of Mozart's 25th Symphony, a tune so successfully used in Titan's television ad campaigns, while his colleagues gave him a standing ovation.

There were more surprises in store with the screening of *Hi Xerxes*, a film featuring people who had known Xerxes from his school days up until his time in Titan, all recalling happy memories. As each one on screen began with a 'Hi Xerxes', everyone in the audience could see how deeply Xerxes was moved. There was Shiamak Marshall, a schoolmate from St. Mary's School whom the team had tracked down in Mumbai. There was Mani Ayer of O&M, Alyque Padamsee of Lintas and several others, all expressing their fondness and admiration for Xerxes Desai. Film-maker Rajiv Menon, whose classic ad for Titan watches showing a father gifting a watch to his daughter on her wedding day while the other daughter played the Mozart tune on the piano was a huge hit, delivered a recorded tribute to Xerxes. This was especially poignant for Xerxes as he had initially had misgivings about the efficacy of this television commercial.

While rock star Remo Fernandes performed a song especially composed for Xerxes, there was a message from Tata Sons' Chairman Ratan Tata placing on record his appreciation of Xerxes's work.

After the videos and the speeches and the dinner, many of the Titanians who came from other cities, partied all night and headed straight for the airport the next morning. The Titan family, even those who had moved out of the company, was one that built lifelong bonds.

On Xerxes's last official day at the office, the Titan team ensured that the lift fetching him to his sixth floor office stopped on every floor and when the lift door opened, he was cheered and feted and handed bouquets by the entire staff on that floor. In the evening, the entire Titan team gathered on the ground floor of the Titan office at Golden Enclave to applaud him as he left the office one last time in his trademark white shirt, folded at the cuff. With that, on Monday, 1 April 2002, the era of Xerxes Desai came to an end, and a new one began, that of Titan's second MD, Bhaskar Bhat.

EIGHT

ON THE FASTRACK

I.K. Amitha was horrified. He held the sample watch that his product manager, Kalpana Kar, was showing him: it was a colourful plastic affair, lightweight, with detachable straps and a dial which showed a design in three cube shapes of blue, red and yellow. Then he picked up a solid steel watch. 'Look at this watch, Kalpana,' Amitha said. 'You can feel its weight. This is something you can pass on to your children. What's this flimsy thing you are throwing in my face?' As Titan's senior vice president (the year was 1991, he passed away in 1999), and a man with a special interest in the manufacturing process, he was understandably perturbed. For him, a good watch was a family heirloom to be passed on from parents to children.

Kalpana laughs, remembering vividly how she argued with Amitha that this 'flimsy thing' would be a style statement for a whole generation. The entire range of Titan watches came with metal cases; introducing plastic casing and straps would mean a radical shift. Nothing like this was available either in the regulated market or among smuggled watches. 'We wanted to launch a fun watch for [the] youth, a segment we were not really addressing.

The rationale was to expand the reach of Titan. When people travelled abroad they would come back with sporty watches like Swatch that caught people's attention,' recalls Kalpana, also a recruit of TAS, in a conversation at her palatial bungalow in Bengaluru's Koramangala area.

Swatch had created a revolution in the global watch market. As an article in the *New York Times* points out, Nicholas Hayek, a Swiss entrepreneur, introduced the Swatch in 1983: 'Lightweight, with vibrantly colored bands and breezy novelty faces, it was remarkably inexpensive to produce. [It had 51 components, as opposed to the nearly 100 needed to make a contemporary wristwatch.] It retailed for less than $35 [approximately ₹955] when it was first marketed in the United States later that year. The Swatch quickly became a sought-after collector's item worldwide. It was very likely the first time that ordinary people had even considered owning multiple watches.'

Swatch was breaking the mould of how watches were viewed until then. It was responding to the tastes of a younger generation. Plastic as a material was coming of age; it was versatile and allowed for the use of vibrant colours and printing, as a result of which the face of the watch itself was changing. Sporty watches were getting tougher; there were waterproof watches for divers and shockproof watches for sports people. Titan needed to keep in step with these trends.

In the watch industry, as with any consumer-goods sector, the threat of competition is ever-present. Therefore, Titan had always to be wary of HMT and Allwyn, in particular, among the domestic competitors, especially when it came to marketing and product styling. Allwyn was known for its eponymous refrigerators. 'Everyone had their own estimates about how long it would take for one or both to come back. My own take was about three years for similar watches to appear. What no one suggested was that either of them could come out with something original and shake us out of our comfort zone,' says Anil Manchanda.

That is exactly what Allwyn did in 1990. It introduced a line called 'Trendy' with colourful dials and plastic straps and immediately created a huge buzz. The watches resonated with young people and their sales took off at what seemed a dizzying pace. Over at Titan, this prompted panic – followed by a series of emergency meetings to chalk out a quick response. Enquiries were floated in Hong Kong and Taiwan to source appearance parts. Teams were dispatched to Delhi to enquire of the government about licensing for import of plastic components. However, the government was very clear: no imports of plastic cases or straps.

A team was set up to explore who in India could produce plastic parts with the accuracy and stability levels needed for watches. 'Then suddenly, out of the blue, I got a call from Ashok Vir, the person we had selected and who had turned down our offer, before we hired Bhaskar Bhat as The Watch Project's first executive before Titan started,' recalls Anil. Ashok had, in the intervening years, set up a company that made and marketed clocks; he had diversified into plastic watch cases and was the exclusive supplier to Allwyn. He offered to make them for Titan too. Anil invited him over and he turned up the very next day to meet with Kalpana.

Kalpana, who was one of the first few Microsoft-trained sales managers in India in the mid-1980s, had moved to the US for a few years and returned to Bangalore in 1989. In August of the same year, she took up a marketing role in Titan. Titan had already set a scorching pace in the Indian watch market and the mood was buoyant. Fastrack had been launched along with other brands to present Titan's sporty face. But at that time what they wanted was a watch that would appeal to young people. 'It was all about talking to the youth, which was a larger genre than sport. We wanted to make a fun watch,' says Kalpana. Since Titan was not geared to manufacturing plastic moulds, the team had to look for someone who could supply high-quality plastic cases and straps. Straps were reserved for the small-scale sector, so finding a partner who was willing to experiment and provide straps at the right price was a challenge. That's where Ashok Vir came in.

'There was a big debate with manufacturing. The team wanted to go more high-end with jewel-embellished watches, maybe with a small diamond or a Swarovski crystal, and did not want to go [for] something that was so light and flimsy. But the whole argument was that there was an entire customer set that Titan was not talking to,' says Kalpana.

At that time, Titan was a young company, barely five years old, and had quickly established its brand. This was the first product-related gamble it was taking, allowing somebody else to handle the quality standards that it had set for itself. As these watches would have to be priced lower than Fastrack and other Titan watches, there was the fear that even if several lakh units were sold, there was the likelihood that it would not lend much to the growth and profitability of the company. However, Xerxes recognized the need to reach out to a new segment and he lent his weight to the project. Ravi Kant, head of sales and marketing, also supported the initiative.

There were other misgivings too. As the first real success for the Tata Group where a consumer-facing company was concerned, failure was not an option. 'The risk of failure was embedded at many layers. We could not afford to fail because that would mean we could do only steel, salt and trucks. The Tata brand couldn't be compromised; what if the dials didn't have an appeal or the product failed?' recalls Kalpana. Titan made serious watches and a brand with funky hands and no markings for numbers on the dial defied the idea of a timekeeping device. Titan's ranges had always been designed after considerable market research: a Royale was associated with a wedding or a formal event; an Exacta was a working individual's choice, associated with durability; Fastrack was a fun watch, for leisure.

The Aqura range was launched in August 1991 at a big event in Bombay. The watch came in two sizes with detachable straps and what would be its most popular watch among the many it launched had three squares designed on the centre of the dial, in blue, red and yellow. This watch design was picked for the launch event. 'Aqura was meant to be Titan's foray into a fun and casual segment using plastic and color for the youth; it had interchangeable straps and was sporty and light. This was the value proposition to add and supplement the range,' elaborates Kalpana. 'It also marked the beginning of [a trend] when women started to wear larger dials on their wrists.'

The colour scheme for the launch function was purple. Xerxes's objections – he felt that the colour was associated more with royalty than the young – were overruled. As Kalpana explains, purple represented creativity and energy, the values they wanted the brand to have. Everybody turned up wearing a splash of purple, either on a saree border or a tie! Even Xerxes had a trick up his sleeve: he presented Kalpana with a painting depicting three cubes in different shades of purple!

The launch of Aqura was a huge success and very soon Titan found that it could not produce enough watches. Fastrack was part of the original portfolio of watches launched by Titan, but when Aqura came into the picture, it was overshadowed. To avoid cannibalization, Fastrack took a secondary position and Titan's leisure watches were all branded Aqura. This brought a new edge to Titan's packaging, branding and retail; henceforth, the company was on the lookout for suppliers who could give the brand a trendy new look and feel.

However, all the research that went into the creation of Aqura threw up another interesting option: there was still space in the market for an attractive, traditional, ethnic watch. Thus, Raga entered the market in 1992. A fusion brand, Raga sported motifs on its dials and straps that were a blend of leather and fabric with bits of noble metal as well. 'It was quite clear that if we were talking about the Indian woman, there was something we needed to offer when she was dressed in ethnic clothes,' explains Kalpana. Most women's watches up until then were replicas of styles for men, only smaller in size. Raga was different: it was specially created for women. 'Putting a Ganesha on a Raga dial or printing on leather felt to many like we were making a toy and not a world-class watch. But, the image of or the need for and role of a watch itself was evolving; Aqura and Raga seeded that change in the Indian market,' she explains.

By 2005, though, it was decided that Raga needed a complete product makeover. Revathi Kant, who was then handling Raga explains: 'We did a lot of detailed consumer studies, met many women, homemakers, working women, to understand why women did not wear watches when they dressed up; they wore bangles on both wrists. We came to understand that for a watch to become popular among women it has to be like a piece of jewellery. That was a major insight for us and sparked off the entire design development.'

Based on this insight, a new design language was developed for Raga, with innovative case shapes, bracelets and bangle watches, all of which looked like jewellery. Raga stood out from other women's watches in the market. 'It wasn't easy to create those kinds of watches, but it gave Raga an identity. Sensuality was another key theme surrounding the Raga collection,' says Revathi. This theme influenced both product design and advertising. The proportions of each watch were such as to make it look sensual; the advertising was also steeped in sensuality.

The Raga line stayed with Titan for several years and underwent many reinventions. Eventually, it was launched as a sub-brand of Titan, positioned as an expression of femininity with the tagline: 'It makes me more of the woman I am'. In 2008 actor Rani Mukherjee was roped in as brand ambassador and the design philosophy moved towards theme-based collections every year – Diva, Aqua, Flora, Chocolat and Espana. Diva was an ornate collection, quite dressy, and used enamel and stone for the first time, all calculated to make the wearer feel like a diva. Aqua was inspired by water, with fluid forms while Flora took its inspiration from flowers. Espana, a more recent collection, has a contemporary look and feel. Each collection featured between 30 and 50 watches, and drew from a variety of Indian experiences and motifs, including the Taj Mahal.

How the team drew inspiration for its designs is an interesting story in itself, as Revathi explains. In one instance she and her design team were at a handmade-chocolate factory near the airport in Bangalore where the owner demonstrated how chocolate is made and then left them to their own devices. The team had a great deal of fun making chocolates. 'After that visit, we sat and tried to hit on a signature element [for the watches] and we zeroed in on the moment when the chocolate melts. That became the theme for a collection called Raga Chocolat. The collection itself, unfortunately, didn't do very well, but it's an example of how we immerse ourselves in the creative process,' says Revathi. Today, Raga is a significant ₹300-crore brand in Titan's portfolio.

Meanwhile, with the advent of Timex, the marketing of Titan Aqura was handed over to the new joint venture it had forged with Timex. Through the rest of the 1990s, Fastrack took a backseat while Titan forayed into jewellery, and focused on going overseas and on Brand Titan itself. In the early 2000s, Fastrack was extended to sunglasses. Ajoy Chawla was given charge of this project. While Fastrack continued as a sub-brand in the watches portfolio, sunglasses under the same brand were launched by a separate team. Sunglasses as a product line was being considered as early as 2000 but made its entry as a pilot project in 2002–03. As a category it was seen as a natural sub-brand extension for Fastrack due to its fashion and style orientation. Market mapping and some consumer research was done to identify the areas a new player like Titan could get into. 'We did a pilot in Bangalore to validate our understanding and fine tune the approach,' recalls Ajoy. Fashion jewellery was also considered but did not progress as the company did not see adequate traction for a potential business in its initial pilots.

Ajoy, who would go on to be senior vice president for strategy and business incubation, says the idea was to get into non-traditional outlets apart from department stores and the hundreds of exclusive Titan outlets across the country. Launching from Bangalore, Ajoy and his team placed the sunglasses in beauty and wellness chains such as Health & Glow, and music stores such as Planet M – apart from, of course, Shopper's Stop and Lifestyle. Surprisingly, the sunglasses didn't initially make any headway in the Tata-owned Westside chain. 'This went to show that we had to make business sense for each store whether it was a Tata chain or otherwise,' says Ajoy. Based on the success of the launch, Ajoy drew up a business plan for the following year and it was decided to take the brand to Mumbai.

'Unfortunately, we ended up launching during the monsoons,' recalls Ajoy, 'and we realized we were total novices.' The overcast skies and incessant rains meant not many were buying sunglasses. The business plan was in shreds and the numbers were nothing compared to the sales notched up in Bangalore. 'I realized that I would at best achieve only 30 per cent of the targeted sales in Mumbai. So I called my team members and told them that the numbers looked bleak. One of them, Nirmal Lobo, who was a sales officer then, said we should try institutional sales. I wondered if it would work for sunglasses,' says Ajoy.

They had set up standees for Fastrack glasses in Titan outlets despite the poor supply mainly because Ajoy knew all the franchisees from his days in marketing at Titan. However, that upset the then retail head of Titan. 'Our sales target that year [2005] was 40,000 units and we had barely sold 10,000 with half the year gone and I had great hopes that through institutional sales and other efforts we could bridge the gap,' Ajoy says, adding that he chewed on this problem while on a one-and-a-half hour flight to Mumbai from Bangalore for a meeting with the sales staff.

Ajoy came out of the meeting to discover many missed calls from a former colleague, who then worked for Samsung. 'One of my colleagues is looking for gifting options for the Diwali season for customers. Would you have any interesting products?' she asked Ajoy. Trying not to sound too excited, Ajoy replied that Fastrack had a great range of sunglasses to show. The next thing Ajoy did was to call the sales head of accessories and licensed brands business unit, S. Natarajan, and tell him to take a flight the very next day to Delhi and camp in the Samsung office till they got the order. Nothing came of that meeting and Natarajan returned empty-handed to Bangalore, only to return to Delhi in a couple of weeks. 'He called me back late in the evening saying that there was good news and bad. The good news was that the Samsung order could be way beyond our annual target. The bad news was that they wanted it at ₹400 a piece while our average selling price was ₹1,000,' recalls Ajoy. The further bad news was that Samsung wanted the sunglasses in the next 90 days, whereas the lead time needed was 120 days! Ajoy told Natarajan to work out a deal and asked him what numbers they were looking at. 'When he told me they wanted to buy one-and-a-half lakh sunglasses, I almost fell off my chair!' says Ajoy laughing. They went right ahead and took on the challenge.

There followed a mad scramble. Ajoy asked Dinesh Amitha, who then headed sourcing for the business unit, if he could execute the order. Meanwhile, Natarajan was told to stay put in Delhi till Fastrack had the contract in hand. Dinesh got on the phone with suppliers in Hong Kong and China; the following day he told Ajoy that he would go sit in Hong Kong and make the order happen and the supplies would come in instalments. Much bargaining later, Samsung said that if the price could be settled at ₹375 a piece, the 1.5 lakh order could even exceed 2 lakh. Samsung wanted the sunglasses supplied across the country. Natarajan was sure he could deliver wherever required; Dinesh assured Ajoy he would make it happen on the supply front.

With all this information in hand, the following day, Ajoy called up Bijou Kurien, chief operating officer of the watches and accessories division. 'I told him we were supplying at this price only because of the volumes and we would still make ₹100 per unit after taxes and my year's target would be achieved,' he says. More importantly, Samsung would advertise Fastrack sunglasses and 1.5 lakh customers would get the brand and increase awareness for Fastrack. Bijou agreed and the deal was on. The final order was 2.4 lakh units in three models, spread over eight deliveries across the country. 'It was phenomenal. We made no compromises on quality as it was a credibility test for us in the market. We ended up making money which was surplus to the business plan. And it's because of this order that we survived – otherwise we may have had to close down the business.' recalls Ajoy.

After the successful execution of the order from Samsung, Ajoy wanted to create more brand awareness for Fastrack sunglasses. He wanted to sign on actor John Abraham as a brand ambassador, even though Bijou was not sure if Fastrack needed one in the first year of the brand launch. Eventually Bijou relented to a persistent Ajoy. 'So, I went ahead and signed on John Abraham but the ad film didn't pan out well, so we took only the last 20 seconds of the film and ran this campaign throughout the summer,' says Ajoy. Soon after, Ajoy, confident that Fastrack had earned the right to be nurtured as a brand, moved out of Fastrack sunglasses and licensed brands business (which allows it to retail brands such as Tommy Hilfiger and Police) in 2005 to Titan as business unit head, watches. The stage was set for Fastrack to take another successful turn.

This time, it landed in the hands of the tall and well-built Ronnie Talati who, until then, had been in the finance department at Titan. Fastrack was completely unfamiliar territory for him but it was a challenge he was ready for. Ronnie used to be Xerxes's neighbour in Mumbai. Keen to be economically independent, he had asked Xerxes for a job although he was still studying for his B.Com degree. He was hired in the finance department of Tata Press on a salary of ₹400 a month. He was just 17 at the time. 'I used to attend classes from 7 a.m. to 9.30 a.m. and then take a bus to Prabhadevi where the Tata Press office was,' says Ronnie. After acquiring his degree, he studied law while still working at Tata Press and in April 1986 moved to Bangalore with the founding team of Titan.

After several years in finance, Ronnie wanted a change and had a chat with Bhaskar about a possible move to some other function. Bhaskar promised to think it over and, true to his word, consulted Bijou about Ronnie's request. They had taken note of the fact that at meetings, Ronnie's interventions revealed a sound marketing brain. This prompted Bhaskar to offer Ronnie the chance to head the accessories and licensing business, which Ajoy had handled till then. 'Accessories' was just Fastrack sunglasses then; besides, Titan had taken on the retailing of Tommy Hilfiger watches under licence from the top US brand. Pleasantly surprised by this offer, Ronnie sought a couple of days to think it over. 'I didn't expect them to make this kind of an offer. I was wondering whether after 20 years in finance I would be up to this new assignment.' He then came back to Bhaskar and Bijou with a counter-proposal. 'You're offering me this small business of sunglasses. But we also have Fastrack watches, so why don't you combine sunglasses and watches and lend some weight to the business?' Ronnie asked them. It was a sensible suggestion and was quickly accepted. 'I didn't even know what my first step should be. Those days we used to sell around two lakh Fastrack watches a year,' recalls Ronnie. The business, along with sunglasses, was around ₹20 crore annually. Now, with both businesses under one head, what Ronnie needed was a good marketing chief and he knew he had to get Simeran Bhasin back to Titan.

Fresh from her MBA from the T.A. Pai Management Institute in Manipal, Karnataka, in 2001, Simeran had joined Titan in sales and was initially posted in Nagpur. Later she moved to marketing at the corporate office in Bangalore, handling sub-brands such as Dash for kids and Fastrack; the top-end Nebula brand was also added to her portfolio. 'It was a schizophrenic existence,' says Simeran recalling her first brief. 'Kids, youth and a luxury watch brand in gold, all at the same time. There was a lot of discussion about what to do with these sub-brands and they were so small that they were always in danger of being dropped. The team around me called me the Assistant Dropped Brands Manager!' recalls Simeran, indignant and amused at the same time. But on the plus side there were intense brainstorming sessions on Fastrack and what its profile should be. The debate swirled around whether Fastrack should target a younger segment than the audience it had been focusing on up until then. Should Fastrack set its sights on 15 to 21 year olds? As was the practice, Simeran along with Manoj Tadepally, then marketing head for Titan, undertook several consumer immersion studies. Esprit, deemed aspirational by the youth, had just come to India, and at the lower end were a slew of Chinese watches. 'There was this big yawning gap in the middle where we saw an opportunity to have international designs at Indian prices,' says Simeran.

The image of a watch was pretty much entrenched in people's minds: they were regular, round or square, with different-coloured straps, and that was it. Simeran suggested that Fastrack be positioned as a fashion accessory and as such, the watches in this collection 'should not look like what a watch looks like'. Award-winning designer Michael Foley who headed Titan's design studio was quick to see the potential in this suggestion, and he and his team came up with fabulous ideas, drawing inspiration from clothing to bikes and even science fiction. Designs flowed, inspired even by spaghetti straps and halter necks in the watches for girls. 'They sold really well and were some of the most distinctive girls' watches in the country for many years,' says Simeran.

Simultaneously, the marketing team worked on the design-to-cost exercise and discussed with the manufacturing team which was, understandably, horrified that they would have to produce complex watch shapes. 'We were given a free hand to develop the brand. So we brought in this concept that Fastrack could be representative of metropolitan India. We took street style as a theme once. Simple things like a manhole on the road became the design for the back cover of a watch; or we would use that pattern to make dials. We even looked at an automotive line. We didn't look at watch designs alone but at furniture, signage, benches et al.; it was just sensibilities of new age cities,' explains Michael.

Keeping in tune with the target audience, the prices had to be reduced. Fastrack sold at ₹1,700 a piece on average; this needed to be slashed to ₹1,200. Manufacturing head Shantharam said his team would take it up as a challenge. So, even as zany watches were being conjured and produced, much more had to be done to project the brand as fun and irreverent. This is also when Fastrack's 'claw' logo was born. On the advertising front, Simeran observed that so far the brand had moved from campaign to campaign – that is, one thought outlined in one campaign before moving on to another in the next campaign. She felt it was time to change this strategy. She felt Fastrack needed one powerful thought that would stay for at least three years if not longer and that would more effectively imprint the brand in consumers' minds.

The positioning Fastrack embarked on has endured to this day, proving its relevance and validity. Saucy, iconoclastic, edgy, imbued with innuendo and often overtly sexual – the ad campaigns for Fastrack have been all this and more. However, the one that defined the new-look Fastrack was the 'Yes Sir' campaign. It has students responding to the roll call in a college classroom. When a cute guy wearing a Fastrack watch raises his hand to answer, a girl pipes up and says 'Yes Sir'; she is followed by another girl who says 'Oh! Yes Sir!' and another and another until the last girl's 'Yes Sir' comes practically in a state of sexual rapture and the teacher is left wondering what's happening to his class! 'He doesn't get it, but the kids do. The innuendo was perfect because you know this is not rebellious but playful irreverence,' explains Simeran. She also felt Fastrack's older tagline – 'Keep Collecting' – didn't strike an emotional chord. Its advertising agency Lowe then came up with the grammatically incorrect but instantly effective 'How many you have?'

'That was perfect, you know, collect fans, admirers, boyfriends and watches too! It worked beautifully at the product level because Fastrack needed to bring out new watches constantly and we needed people to buy multiple watches,' says Simeran. She even parked herself over three days outside Bangalore's Christ College and played the ad on her laptop and was pleasantly surprised that almost all the students had seen the ad and were talking about it. The watches too were flying off the shelves.

Having seen what she could do with Fastrack, Simeran was on a roll. She felt Fastrack did not receive the attention it deserved and she, along with a multi-functional team that Bijou had put together, came up with a more ambitious business plan for the brand. It envisaged the opening of Fastrack cafes with music where young people could hang out and where they could also buy

Fastrack merchandise. 'I identified a retail space in Koramangala in Bangalore for a possible Fastrack store,' recalls Simeran. The plan involved Fastrack having its own sales and marketing team; and it projected that in three years it could hit ₹50 crore in revenue. It had at the time stagnated at ₹25 crore in sales.

Unfortunately, this plan was put on the backburner. It wasn't surprising, therefore, that when Britannia made her an offer to join its dairy division, Simeran accepted. 'Every MBA marketing kid dreams of the FMCG industry as the Mecca of marketing so it was too good to be true and it was in Bangalore,' says Simeran, who quit Titan in July 2005, two weeks after the 'Yes Sir' campaign went on air

Ronnie had moved to head Fastrack a couple of months after Simeran quit Titan. One of the first things he did was to call Simeran. Over a two-hour lunch at the Karnataka Golf Association's clubhouse Simeran poured her heart out. 'I never knew Ronnie as he didn't speak much at our meetings with finance except to say that we were spending too much on advertising!' she says. But this Ronnie was the exact opposite. He told her that Bijou had restructured the watch business into separate business units and that included Fastrack which would also have its own sales team. That day Ronnie talked and talked, enough to convince Simeran to have a conversation with Bijou and rejoin Fastrack as its marketing manager. 'I told her that I had great plans for the brand and wanted to ramp it up from a ₹25 crore to a ₹500 crore business in three years and that she would be given a free hand,' recalls Ronnie.

The first step was to spell out a vision for the brand. The target focus too was changed from the 'early jobbers' to the college-going segment, in the 18 to 25 years age group. 'We wanted to have an independent identity for Fastrack as [at] that time we were still functioning within Titan showrooms with separate Fastrack counters,' says Ronnie.

Still, a separate store with just watches and sunglasses didn't make sense; Fastrack needed more. What could that be? Apparel and footwear were not viable categories because there would not be much differentiation. Around that time, Ronnie and Simeran travelled to Hong Kong for a watch fair, where they bumped into a friend of Ronnie's, Sanjiv Bulchandani, who was in leather goods and had launched a brand called Bulchis. Making small talk in the atrium of the watch fair, Sanjiv said he had launched bags, belts and wallets. Ronnie and Simeran looked at each other. 'What do you think, Simeran?' Ronnie asked. 'I said, "Sounds exciting!" and at that moment, standing with Sanjiv, we took a decision to launch bags, belts and wallets under Fastrack,' recalls Simeran. He said he even had the right brand manager for them: Komal Jyoti, a designer with the leather goods brand Hidesign, who wanted to move from her current job to marketing. It was an impulsive decision, recalls Simeran, to move a designer into brand management. However, they reasoned, consumer focus is a key part of a designer's training and Simeran was sure Komal could come up with creative ideas for the brand. 'The decision to move into bags was right as at that time there were a few luggage brands but they were not big on bags and backpacks; there seemed to be a wide open space for us to get into,' explains Ronnie. Sanjiv said he would be able to supply all the products.

Fastrack did not have a designer for bags and belts at that time so Komal doubled up in that role. Sanjiv directed Ronnie, Simeran and Komal to Guangzhou in China, which had a huge inventory of whatever they needed. There, they headed straight for the huge buildings that housed the bag markets and picked up an enormous number of samples, over a hundred pieces at least. They picked up loads of fabric as well and went back to Ronnie's room. Komal's mind had already started ticking and she got on to her laptop right away to design the entire range that could constitute the initial launch. 'The sample bags were used as references for individual elements that we liked – the shape in some, the trims in another, and a new look was put together by Komal,' explains Simeran. 'We stapled fabric and trims to the various sample bags and handed it to Sanjiv's team to have prototypes made – and we loved what came out,' says Simeran.

Now, with enough accessories to fill a store, the team, which had also roped in Hemal Panchamia, the brand manager for sunglasses, zeroed in on Pune as the city which would have the first Fastrack store. Ronnie, Simran and Hemal visited a number of potential stores to rent in Pune. One was right outside the renowned Fergusson College, above a Barista outlet. 'We walked up and down that road and felt a buzz around the place; we looked at it and said this is it,' recalls Simeran. Michael Foley, who had by then left Titan to set up his own studio, was roped in to design the store. It would have to be very different from the exclusive, elitist Titan and Tanishq stores, where everything was displayed in glass cases and kept under lock and key. In the Fastrack stores, young people would be encouraged to see, touch and feel the products. The Pune store, all of 350 square feet, opened in February 2009.

In fact, the profile of the Fastrack team actually resembled the consumer target group for this brand – most of them were in their mid-20s, fun-loving and eager to challenge the status quo. Ronnie, at 40 plus, was perhaps the only exception. They occupied an entire floor at Golden Enclave, the erstwhile headquarters in Bangalore, and even played table tennis right in the middle of the room! Needless to say, they dressed quite differently from everyone else in the building.

Along with the opening of its first store, Fastrack signed on two fast-rising stars – the bubbly actor Genelia D'Souza and cricketer Virat Kohli, who would eventually be appointed captain of India's cricket team. Saucy ads broke out on television of the pair canoodling in an ATM and another of Genelia gently flirting with the staff at an airport check-in counter, Virat in tow.

'Introducing Fastrack bags, move on!' said the tagline. Brand consultant Santosh Desai implemented a seminal consumer insight project for Fastrack around 2006 and through this project played a key role in evolving Fastrack's new proposition which was encapsulated in the words 'Move on'. This became a sort of anthem for Fastrack. The tag line, Simeran explains, came from the insight that young people liked owning things in multiple numbers and in having a multiplicity of experiences. 'The idea was that instead of being rooted in the past, youth had to move on from their comfort zone, indulge in new experiences, and move on to the next, and take opportunities that came their way. It's "move on" in a positive sort of way,' she explains.

The ads set the market on fire. The store rapidly notched up sales of ₹2.5 crore in its first year. Simeran says marketers make much of location being the key to a store's success. The Pune store was bang on. They did not need to spend money to promote the store as Fergusson College Road (or FC Road, as it's popularly known) shoppers kept streaming in from day one! 'It was magical,' she exclaims. In fact, it remains one of Fastrack's top five stores in the country to date. In the first year of Fastrack's retail foray, a few more stores rapidly came up – in Chennai, Hyderabad and Bangalore – all successful. Over the next four years, Fastrack scaled up to 100 stores. Fastrack was always projected as separate from Titan or the Tata Group. Neither are mentioned anywhere in the Fastrack stores. 'Both brands were seen as being staid and for older people, so Fastrack deliberately positioned itself as a separate brand. There was a lot of positive feedback and some negative too. Some people even thought we were a foreign brand which was showing a lot of sex in its advertising,' says Ronnie with a hearty laugh. Fastrack had an ad which started with 'F★★K' and Ronnie had people calling from Bombay House saying that they were impacting Tata's brand image! If Bhaskar didn't like the Fastrack ad, he would say so, and also add that if he didn't like it then it must be good, as he wasn't the target audience. Lowe, the advertising agency that helped develop advertising for Tanishq, was also doing the campaigns and communication for Fastrack. As if reflecting the 'generation gap', inevitably, sparks would fly at Fastrack-Lowe meetings!

Each time a Fastrack advertisement appeared, there would be two distinct sets of reactions – on the one hand a series of congratulatory messages hailing Fastrack for charting a new creative path, and another angry set of messages questioning the propriety of the advertisements. The Fastrack team reported to Harish Bhat, then the chief operating officer of the watches division. 'The Fastrack team was a bunch of immensely talented, passionate young boys and girls, led by an equally young-at-heart Ronnie. What brought them together was their instinctive shared understanding of what college-going youth in urban India wanted to wear, see, do and talk about. Ronnie and his team dedicated themselves to translating this understanding into bold watch designs, equally striking store formats, and advertising campaigns that stood out by a mile. They spoke the language of their consumers all the time, often much to the discomfort of people with a more conservative mindset. The team knew they had to walk on the edge very carefully, and tastefully, and I think they did that very successfully most of the time, breaking new ground again and again,' explains Harish.

From its existing product range of watches, bags and backpacks, Fastrack has now launched helmets and looks to launching other motorcycle riding gear as well. The store design too has undergone a change. Designers from the Bangalore-based design house, Praxis, tasked with developing a new design in 2011, were literally tearing their hair as the Fastrack team rejected over 50 of their suggestions. 'Just give us something irreverent,' Ronnie finally told them. And irreverent is what they got. The refurbished store – five as of 2018 – is a jungle of poles on which the products are strung, bird cages serve as displays, hands hanging from the ceiling hold up the bags, mannequins are all wrapped in belts. 'The office bag is dead; today even senior executives carry backpacks and we would like to think that we brought about that change in India,' says Ronnie.

Fastrack pioneered the use of digital marketing when digital in India was still in its early days because it realized that that's where college-going youth were hanging out. It was one of the first Indian brands to notch up 10 million fans on Facebook. In the early days, its in-house digital marketing team consisted of a couple of college-going interns and thereafter, a young full-time executive. Now, of course, it uses a digital agency.

Starting out with selling two lakh watches a year with a turnover of ₹20 crore, Fastrack today sells over 4 million watches, over a million pairs of sunglasses and over half-a-million bags and accessories each year. With 170 stores in total, the Fastrack brand in financial year 2017–18 registered sales of ₹1,200 crore. After a good run in Titan, both Simeran and Ronnie took a leaf out of Fastrack's tagline and moved on. Simeran quit in March 2014 to join outdoor and adventure product company Wildcraft, and later went on to start her own outfit, Brag, which makes innerwear for teens. Ronnie moved on to head the eyewear business of Titan. He didn't 'tire of life on the Fastrack' he says, he only wanted a new challenge.

What was the recipe for the success of India's most admired youth brand? Harish Bhat has a simple answer: 'They were true to their target consumers. It was the total immersion in their consumers that created the Fastrack magic. I saw my own role as providing broad strategic direction to Fastrack, ensuring that business metrics were met, and, most importantly, providing this maverick team all the space they needed to stay the course and to work at their most fluent, creative best. Which they did!'

NINE

LIVING ON THE EDGE

B.G. Dwarakanath had always had an abiding interest in tinkering with micro-precision equipment. Even while he was in college, his hobby was to repair clocks and cameras. After he acquired his engineering degree, to his great delight he was offered a job in the premier machine tools company of the 1970s and 1980s, HMT. 'I had an offer from the machine tools division but chose to join the watch division of HMT as my heart lay in watch design,' recalls the diminutive Dwarak, who joined Titan's founding team in 1985. His deep interest in precision technology would later drive Dwarak to spearhead the development of the world's slimmest watch movement (the interior timekeeping elements of a watch) with a dedicated team of engineers and lead to the launch of Titan's blockbuster brand, Edge. This, then, is the story of Titan Edge.

Ever since watch-making emerged as a craft first and then as an industry, watchmakers have striven to excel at design, from the slimmest watch, also by definition the simplest, to the 'grand complication' watches that sell for hundreds of thousands of dollars. Watch fashions keep changing but there has always been a market for cutting edge designs. In the 1970s and early 1980s, with the emergence of electronic analogue timekeeping, there was a race to make the slimmest quartz watch. The leaders were the Swiss company Ebauches S.A. at the top, followed by the German manufacturer Bifora and America's Timex.

Bifora had made a few such watches in the early 1980s in its German plant but gave up because of quality issues and poor battery life. Bifora also had an Indian arm which made wristwatches and clocks on a small scale. This part of their business was run by its Indian distributors who had got a manufacturing licence to commercialize it. The Bifora plant was in Electronic City on Hosur Road on the outskirts of Bangalore.

Anil Manchanda's wife, Kusum, happened to meet Jawahar Kandhari, the owner of Bifora, in connection with advertising in the *Reader's Digest*. As it turned out, Jawahar's nephew, Rahul, was in school with the Manchandas' son, Alok. Professional connections extended to social interactions and the Manchandas and Kandharis soon became friends and often met socially without ever discussing business or watches.

'One day, as we were enjoying a drink at the Bangalore Club, Jawahar invited me to stop by on the way to Hosur and visit his factory. I accepted and later that week, accompanied by Claude Gaudot, our technical advisor, along with Dwarakanath, I visited Bifora. The plant was rather more impressive than I had visualized based on similar visits to other small-scale factories,' recalls Anil. Anil was particularly intrigued by the 'movement design cell'. In this section, a designer called P. Subramanya Bhat was leading an effort to adapt the German slim watch design to Indian conditions, using limited manufacturing equipment that had seen earlier service in Germany.

'Bhat was not making much progress. I spoke to Dwarakanath and asked him if he would like to lead an effort to create a slim movement for Titan. He jumped at the opportunity,' says Anil.

As it turned out, Dwarak knew Bhat and was familiar with his work. Anil suggested that Dwarak speak to Bhat and see if he would like to do in Titan what he was doing in Bifora but with much greater access to resources. Bhat, who had first worked with Hegde and Golay, a company that Titan had once tried to acquire, jumped at the opportunity. 'For me, having earlier worked at Bifora in Germany under a Swiss engineer had helped a lot and in turn [helped me to] establish contacts in Switzerland. At Titan it was a free hand and support from the top,' Bhat recalls.

Meanwhile, Gaudot was enlisted to locate a design expert in Europe to vet and guide the efforts of the Titan team. That person was Weilly Meyer. 'Since successful original or even adapted movement design was at best a long shot, I did not even bother to consult anyone else before green-lighting the project,' recalls Anil. With Dwarak as team leader, Bhat in charge of research and development (R&D) along with V. Nellaiyappan, Suresh Madhbavi and S.K. Prakash, the team set out to meet the challenge of designing a slim movement.

Working in Titan was a fetters-free experience. In the early days, for instance, the manufacturing team led by Amitha had only to explain to Xerxes and Anil whatever equipment they required and why, and it was immediately made available. Amitha once summed it up saying, 'Titan is HMT plus improvements, less mistakes.' That's how Dwarak got the approval for Titan's first computer numerically controlled (CNC) machine. 'Xerxes and I were travelling together by car. I had the proposal ready and as we got out of the car on to the pavement I told him I needed his clearance. He said, "Why are you preaching to the converted?" [The machinery] was priced at a landed cost of ₹2 crore; Xerxes merely said, "You want my autograph?" and signed the proposal on the car bonnet. He didn't really read the document, that was the level of trust,' recalls Dwarak. Hari Rao, the general manager of the Hosur factory (including the engineering design department), comfortably purchased expensive auto-CAD machines for computer-aided drawing and design. When Titan established an assembly plant in Dehradun, all that Shantharam and Dwarak had to do was call the equipment and machinery suppliers as soon as the land for the factory was identified; the plant was set up in a record 45 days. There was neither red-tape nor bureaucratic rigmarole, nor was there an occasion for arguments or justifications.

The thickness of the standard watch movements being made by Titan with the technical collaboration of France Ebauches ranged from 2.6mm to 3.5mm. By 1992, the transfer of technology was complete and Titan's production team was surpassing the quality standards of its French collaborator. The first proposal for the development of a slim movement that the team of engineers led by Bhat at Titan came up with in 1993 featured a round-shaped movement that was 1.75mm thick with a diameter of 19.7mm (or, in watch industry lingo, 8¾ lignes; lignes is a watch movement measure where 1 ligne is equal to 2.25mm) compared to the 2.6mm thick movement, the slimmest movement that Titan had so far made with the technical inputs of France Ebauches. 'It was slim. We could have made a watch under 4mm, but everyone wanted a slimmer watch,' recalls Bhat. But, as Dwarak says, the development period was long as the new development had to depend on existing processes.

The R&D team was given a free hand to develop the slim movement, code-named 9092, and Xerxes was pleased with the prototype. However, the team encountered unexpected opposition from the marketing department, which believed the market did not need slim movements of 1.75mm thickness and a 20mm diameter. Marketing felt the need was only for thick watches. A stormy meeting followed, at the end of which Xerxes finally said that Titan would stop the development of the slim movement as there appeared to be no requirement for it in the market. 'Naturally, we were shocked by this decision. At this point, Hari Rao said we should develop what the market wants and not what the marketing department wants. He told Xerxes and the marketing team that this product could be positioned well and a market would need to be created for it,' recalls Dwarak.

Dwarak also piped up and told Xerxes, 'I've heard of abortion before birth, but this is the first time I am hearing of abortion after birth.' Although Dwarak's impudence took Xerxes by surprise, he mulled over the matter for a few minutes and then gave the green signal to the team. 'This is how the fortunes of R&D in Titan changed,' adds Dwarak.

Encouraged by this decision, the R&D team took the initiative to simultaneously develop a movement for women, code-named 9086; it was 5½ x 6¾ lignes in size and had a thickness of 2mm. The development of these two movements was completed in 1995 and Titan was ready to introduce slim watches into the market. The fact that its top-of-range collection using slim movements, Classique, continues to be a hit is proof of its popularity. Further endorsement came in 1996 in the form of an award for R&D from the Department of Scientific and Industrial Research, the Ministry of Science and Technology, Government of India. The recognition of their efforts was hugely encouraging for the team. Xerxes pumped them up further to work towards creating an even slimmer movement than what the Swiss and Japanese had made thus far by asking the team: 'What's the purpose of creating such a movement? Is it just to create history? We should create a movement and a watch that will be of high quality and reliability, and not just something for a museum. It should also be affordable.'

The team then began to collect data on various watch movements from across the world. 'We found out that Citizen of Japan had made a movement with a thickness of 0.98mm, but it was very expensive for a watch. Concord of Switzerland had developed a watch called Delirium with a mechanism built into the back cover resulting in a watch of 2mm thickness. Bifora of Germany also had a similar concept watch with a thickness of 2.7mm. Both Concord and Bifora slim watches, produced in very small quantities, became museum pieces. They were [made] solely for purity of design; mass production would have been difficult. And even if they were to make them, they were so thin that reliability was a big question mark. They were also very delicate,' explains Dwarak.

However, the Titan team was up to the task: they decided to take up the challenge of making an ultra-slim movement in all-metal. For starters, they decided to more than halve the movement thickness, from 2.6mm to 1.15mm, the thickness of a credit card. The reason for this dimension was that the smallest quartz crystal then commercially available was 1mm in diameter and the slimmest battery was 1 mm thick. If they succeeded, it would be the world's slimmest movement to be mass produced and commercialized. To this challenge, Xerxes added another: the watch would have to be water-resistant. After all, argued Xerxes, nobody would want to buy a delicate watch if it couldn't withstand the harsh weather conditions in India.

A special multi-functional team cutting across departments was set up for the project, soon to be christened Edge. There was Bhat from R&D, B.V. Nagaraj from new product development, Azeez Khan from movement manufacturing, Rafeekh Ahmed from case manufacturing, N.V. Narayan from purchase, Srinivas Naik from quality assurance and Michael Foley from product design. 'We were collectively supposed to drive the development and report directly to Xerxes. So, every sketch I made I used to show to him,' recalls Michael.

Since Xerxes's heart was in the design and aesthetics of Titan's product offerings, Michael, who had trained at the National Institute of Design, Ahmedabad, had been working very closely with him, especially when designing the jewellery watch line for

Tanishq. 'I used to place my designs at a distance so that he could see the proportions correctly. Working with Xerxes was very interesting, and I was fortunate to be exposed to his perspective. And that helped in all my first lines, especially the one I did for Edge. Attention to detail was another thing I learned there,' says Michael. Xerxes was always fond of saying, 'god is in the detail.'

The challenge in watch design, says Michael, is how to fit all the design ideas into a two-inch space. With Edge, the main sensibility was the movement; the more elaborate the design, the thicker the watch would get. 'So, my [focus] was on how to make the watch lighter so that when you wear it you can actually forget that there's something strapped on your wrist,' says Michael. He made a whole lot of sketches; one of the designs was for the case to be done in glass but the existing technology didn't support this idea. So stainless steel it had to be. 'The challenge was to design the watch and then to make sure that there was a manufacturing space to build a viable watch, capable of production. It was an iterative process – you design a product and then you "engineer it out". There are challenges at the engineering end as to how to make the designed product and that process goes through many evolutions,' he explains. It wasn't easy: it took four years to complete the design.

The other challenge, Dwarak points out, was changing the mindset of the team. After all, if the Swiss couldn't do it, how could a Titan team succeed? Everything had to be miniaturized and compressed. Some of the existing equipment in the factory had to be upgraded or freshly procured to make the parts required for the slim movement. 'We had a good tool room which could support us very well. All the tools were new and freshly made as everything had to be synced to the new dimensions. Everything was a new part, not a single part was from old stock,' says Bhat. Well, they had not reckoned with the extent of encouragement they would be given, particularly from Xerxes.

Apart from the battery needing special attention, all the components had to be slim as well, including the battery. Initially, Titan sourced a 1mm-thick battery from Union Carbide, but it was very expensive and of low life. The customer couldn't be expected to change the battery every year. The Japanese company Seiko had a much cheaper battery; though it was slightly thicker at 1.2mm, it had a longer life. Since the watch had to be water-resistant, the back cover would need to be removed as infrequently as possible. Therefore, as Dwarak points out, it was important they got a battery with a long life.

Alongside, the Titan team had to also make a thin step-motor to propel the components that drive the hands of a watch. 'The challenge was to keep the step-motor as small as possible and yet have sufficient torque to drive the hands while drawing less energy from the battery,' says Dwarak. Titan worked with a Swiss company, Audemar, to develop the step-motor. It sourced the integrated circuit from Seiko/Epson and matched it with the step-motor. Later, the team indigenized the step-motor, making it more efficient; further improvements made to the integrated circuit resulted in the battery of an Edge watch lasting more than five years!

By year 2000, the R&D team had succeeded in making an ultra-slim movement but the marketing team only reiterated what it had said before: that there was no market for ultra-slim watches. Unfazed, Xerxes decided to develop the movement for the Swiss market; it was called Papillon, French for butterfly, and Dwarak went to Basel to make a pitch for it. He met with representatives from the top Swiss brands such as Raymond Weil, Tissot and Longines. Everyone was impressed, and incredulous too that an Indian company had developed such a slim movement. But the reaction was like a slap in the face. 'I remember the meeting with Raymond Weil officials who were quite excited about our movement but left it to a senior member to take a call. He saw our movement and sarcastically asked me if I knew the prices of Raymond Weil watches and the prices of the movements they used. When I said yes, he further asked if I expected them to use an Indian movement to save some money and dilute their strong brand name!' recalls Dwarak. That is when Dwarak, even though he felt humiliated, realized what brand power meant. This story of Dwarak's encounter with Raymond Weil did the rounds in the Titan stall and at the end of the day, he was at the receiving end of jovial taunts by colleagues asking how many movements he had sold that day.

Chastened, Dwarak and his team returned to Bangalore and the ultra-slim movement hung fire for over a year till Xerxes decided to use the movement to launch a line of watches that would eventually be branded 'Titan Edge'. Since Titan's attempts to get the Swiss to use the ultra-slim movement in their watches had failed, Xerxes decided that Titan would take up the challenge of making an ultra-slim watch on its own.

This was easier said than done. First of all, who would make an ultra-slim case for an ultra-slim movement? Dwarak and Nagaraj flew to Switzerland to meet with manufacturers there but no one was ready to make a case to such exacting specifications, and water-resistant at that. Refusing to give up, Xerxes and Hari Rao then took the call to manufacture everything in-house.

Rafeekh Ahmed, who was part of the core team, was initially skeptical. How would they make a case of just 3.5mm thickness compared to the industry standard of nearly 5mm? But he was eventually convinced by Hari Rao and Dwarak to come on board. The fact that even the Swiss had not attempted to do this may have been something of a motivation. For the first set of Edge watches, the team made various drawings that did not meet with Xerxes's expectations. So, the design and prototype team made various-shaped coins in brass each curved differently. Xerxes inspected them minutely, even checking the reflection of light on the curves and he finally chose one, based on which the final case was made.

Michael remembers the sequence of trial and error that went into getting the watch sapphire crystal right. Regular glass couldn't be ground down to make the slim sheet required; it would shatter. So they opted for the more expensive but sturdier sapphire glass. 'We ground it down to a level where we could still establish the diameter and thickness to a threshold where it didn't shatter. At that time, the thickness of sapphire glass we used for our expensive watches was in the region of 1mm but for Edge we had to push it down to 0.3mm. It was quite a task,' he explains.

That wasn't all: every single component had to be tweaked to the requirements of ultra-slim. A normal dial, which is the face of the watch, is 0.4mm thick; this was reduced to 0.3mm by working with the dial supplier, Kamala Dials, based in Chandigarh. The dial is fashioned from a thin brass sheet upon which are fixed the indices, and other details such as the brand name are printed. The watch hand is usually 120–150 microns thick; in this instance, the hands had to be brought down to just 100 microns, only slightly thicker than a human hair. Even the leather straps had to be whittled down in thickness. In other watches, the back cover has two projections that fit perfectly into matching notches on the case. For Edge, a groove was made all round the watch case and a very thin gasket inserted into it to ensure that the back cover sat snug and the watch was sealed well enough to be water-resistant.

Assembling the ultra-thin watch entailed a great deal of attention to detail. Eventually, Titan spent a tidy ₹4 crore for the development work to create a watch only 3.5mm thick. The 20 or so prototypes in different shapes and designs were put through scores of tests to see how they reacted to low and high temperatures, vibrations, magnetic fields, exposure to ultra-violet rays, the works. They were thrown into a body of water and allowed to remain there for half an hour; they were dropped from a height of one metre on to a hard wooden board to test impulse resistance; they were made to run on 1.35 volts for 24 hours as against the standard 1.55 volts. The ultimate test was done by Dwarak who tied two watches to the front shaft of his car's shock absorber and drove several times between Bangalore and Hosur. He tested five different watches, driving over 200 km in all. Edge survived the bad roads as well.

After the watches had passed all these tests, the prototypes were sent to a horological certifying lab in Switzerland, Chronofiable S.A., which again subjected the watches to the same tests over several weeks. Once again they came through with flying colours, even proving to be sufficiently water-resistant. For watches, Dwarak explains, water-resistance is measured by the pressure that a watch can withstand. Pressure at surface level would be 1 atmosphere of 1 kg/sq. cm and the index of atmospheric pressure increases by 1 kg for every 10 metres depth. A watch such as Edge could withstand pressure even while being immersed in water to a depth of 30 metres or a pressure of 3 kg/sq. cm. Edge had finally arrived, with a movement as thin as a credit card and the watch itself thinner than a floppy disk and weighing just 100 grams.

At a pinch, Titan could have sliced off another 0.5mm: it had the capability to make the watch 3mm thick but the battery technology hadn't kept apace. This would have meant that customers would have had to pay at least ₹400 a piece to replace it at regular intervals. 'We made it 3.5mm so that quality, reliability and servicing would be maintained. It was better to make a 3.5mm watch as rugged as a regular watch than making it flimsy and asking customers to be careful,' says Dwarak.

Edge was launched in Bangalore on 23 May 2002 in 13 variants, eight in stainless steel and five in plated versions. The variants were priced between ₹4,495 and ₹4,995, the most expensive watches from Titan at the time. When Edge came into the market, Titan had to show in its advertising that it had indeed launched the world's slimmest watch. Bijou Kurien recalls that in every ad, on television, in print ads and in the window displays – everywhere – the watch was shown sideways apart from face-up. 'The main driver of Edge was its slimness and we couldn't demonstrate that showing only the front,' explains Bijou. And the front showed that it was not just slim but attractive as well. To drive home the point, one of Edge's launch parties had slim models dressed in costumes that tapered off like fins.

Apart from taking it to the Basel fair, Titan also invited mediapersons from international horological magazines to visit Bangalore and write about Edge. The government bought over 300 pieces to gift to visiting foreign dignitaries as an example of Indian precision engineering. It was the talking point at all of Titan's retail events.

Meera Harish recalls Titan's participation in the Shanghai Watch & Clock Trade Fair in the last quarter of 2002. The only question that Chinese visitors to their booth had was: 'Can I buy an Edge watch?' Unfortunately the request had to be turned down because products at a trade fair are not for sale, but it certainly established the fact that Edge had caught everybody's fancy. Of course, as far as the Titan team was concerned, there was also the fear that the Chinese would want to replicate Edge.

Ravi Kant (SRK) recalls selling hundreds of customized Edge watches in 'white gold' to the Emir of Qatar so he could gift them. The 'white gold' cases were made with an alloy of silver, copper and nickel. Efforts were also made within the Tata fold to build the brand: all the CEOs of the Group companies received customized watches to wear. They in turn ordered Edge watches to gift when they travelled abroad. The Tata Group also had a special edition of Edge made with J.R.D.'s signature on it.

From making it first in steel, Titan went on to launch Edge in gold and titanium; the latest is ceramic, priced at ₹23,000. Edge continues to be a bestseller.

'The quality and reliability is in no way inferior to a Swiss-made watch. If you [were to] remove [the] brand [name] Titan and put a Swiss badge on it, I am sure it would sell for a lot more,' says Dwarak wistfully, alluding to the Indian fascination with foreign brands. Titan's Edge showed that it could match up to the best in the world with its precision engineering. Edge won the German Red Dot award for design as well as a prize from the Marico Innovation Foundation for innovative practices. In fact, Edge has consistently been named among the top 50 innovative products to emerge from India since Independence.

In 2003, Titan launched Edge for women; these watches were smaller than those for men. As of July 2018, Titan has sold 1.4 million men's and two lakh women's Edge watches. 'Edge happened because of Xerxes's backing and [the confidence] that developers could take risks without the fear of retribution. It created a culture of innovation in the company. Edge is a great success story for Titan. It was the result of great teamwork,' says Dwarak. He retired as chief operating officer of the precision engineering division in 2010 but continued as a corporate advisor and technical consultant at Titan for another five years.

At the very outset, Amitha had always said Titan should picture itself as a company in the high precision business. The success of Edge and Titan's ability to work with micro-precision equipment laid the foundation for Titan's precision engineering division, spearheaded by Dwarak. It is in the industrial automation solutions space and also makes precision components for the aerospace, automotive and defence industries. The precision components business employs 400 engineers and supplies to companies such as Pratt & Whitney Canada, Hindustan Aeronautics Ltd and Israel Aerospace, among others. As Bhaskar likes to quip,

Titan is a company that makes aircraft parts and also watches! Among the aircraft parts that Titan makes are engine seals, gear box housings, engine impellers and fuel metering and regulator bodies. Its automation solutions business too has grown to a team of 300 engineers and offers special purpose assembly and testing solutions to a variety of industries ranging from automotive to transportation and consumer packaged goods. With both these businesses growing, they were hived off into a separate company called Titan Engineering and Automation Ltd (TEAL) in 2017, a fully-owned subsidiary of Titan Company Ltd.

More than a decade and a half since Edge was launched, the slim watch continues to provide an edge to Titan's sales. To commemorate the 150th year of the Tata Group in 2018, Titan developed a special edition of Edge featuring on its dial the facsimile of a letter written by the founder of the Tata Group, Jamsetji Tata, to Swami Vivekananda. In this letter, Jamsetji puts forward his vision for the Indian Institute of Science, Bangalore. It is a fitting tribute to the horology traditions that the Tata Group have always honoured.

The Infy Challenge

Sometime towards the end of 2002, Vikram Rajaram, vice president, corporate affairs, got a call from an old acquaintance, N.R. Narayana Murthy (NRN), chairman of Infosys. NRN had a request: his Infoscions traversed the world and they needed a watch which, besides showing the local time, also showed the time in India at a glance. Although dual time watches were available they did not display Indian Standard Time.

The simple reason for this, Vikram explains, is that dual time watches are indexed on longitudes, which are 15 degrees apart. This translates to one hour between each longitude. East of Greenwich (from where Greenwich Mean Time [GMT] is used to calculate clock time across the world), Karachi is five hours ahead and Dhaka, six hours ahead. India being five-and-a-half hours ahead, falls between longitudes and gets bypassed.

Now, NRN wanted a watch indexed on India. Could Titan develop it by April of 2003? The day after he had made the request, two dual time watches he had acquired on his travels were delivered to the Titan office in Bangalore. Vikram passed these on to Dwarak, the go-to person for watch development; Dwarak roped in P.S. Bhat. Some brainstorming later it was decided that since one had to be able to switch between time zones swiftly, the solution had to be a digital watch. Within a few weeks a prototype was ready.

NRN, however, was a stickler for detail, no less than Xerxes used to be. He insisted on going over the profile of the case, the size and the appearance of the LCD numerals, resulting in several iterations and the steady passage of time. There were two concerns, the first was that, vendors who were based in China and Hong Kong would shut down in February for the Chinese New Year, and if orders were not placed well before February, meeting the April deadline would be difficult. The second was that since the components had to be developed, a certain minimum number was required – between 1,500 to 3,000 watches. The team wondered how to break this news to NRN. Meanwhile, Titan came up with something that met NRN's exacting standards, and the latter called in his colleagues Mohandas Pai and Kris Gopalakrishnan to get their approval as well.

As the Titan team tried to figure out how to convey to NRN the minimum quantity he would have to order, the Infosys chairman himself had something to communicate. He announced that in April 2003 Infosys would become a billion dollar company, and to mark this occasion he wanted to gift the 'Infy watch' to each of his employees. All 25,000 of them.

'We were gobsmacked!' says Vikram. But the April 2003 date would hold and Titan had to ensure that Infosys employees all across the globe received the watch on the appointed day. Titan managed to meet the challenge. In fact, this was then among the largest institutional orders Titan had received.

The footnote to this story is that the final order was 25,001 watches, with the last one being presented to Vikram by NRN who also signed his thanks on the wrapper. The watches became a testimony to a culture that encouraged risk, enterprise and innovation.

TEN

BUSINESSES OF THE FUTURE

'So, where do we want to take this company? Do we want to drift into the future or do we want to create a future for ourselves?' These were the questions Bhaskar posed to around 60 middle- and senior-level managers seated in a hall one day in 2004. On screen were projected the total revenues the managers had presented as part of their business plan for the next three years. As far as Bhaskar was concerned, they reflected merely incremental growth. 'Is this our collective ambition?' he asked. 'Is this what we want to be? Do we set our agenda for the future? I want a clear idea of our ambition.'

Rather than draw his own vision for the future of the company, Bhaskar wanted to extract the vision from Titanians themselves. Hence, an exercise eponymously called 'Future Shock' after Alvin Toffler's best-selling 1970 book was designed especially for the Titan team.

Bhaskar Bhat had taken over as managing director in 2002 under trying circumstances, and Titan was only just emerging from the Xerxes Desai era. The balance sheet was weak, Titan was still struggling with the accumulated losses from the failed Europe venture and Tanishq had not yet started raking in significant revenues. Much of the gains from the watch business had gone into fuelling diversifications and that business itself was under pressure. Soon after Bhaskar took over the company was relieved of over 600 employees thanks to a voluntary retirement scheme. In early 2003, the company had had to contend with a 68-day lockout with the workforce striking over a performance-linked wage revision. For Bhaskar, it was baptism by fire. One of the first things Bhaskar did to get Titan back on track was to call in the consultancy firm McKinsey to give advice on operational improvements, driving costs down and growing the business. Once this piece was done, the next step was to define the future vision of the company through an internal process.

Ajoy Chawla, who heads strategy and business incubation for Titan, and Meera Harish, who went on to be the chief operating officer (global business) of leather goods brand Hidesign, worked closely with Bhaskar on Future Shock. 'It was all about capturing our collective imagination and setting a collective goal for the next five years: where do we want to be in terms of topline, bottomline, market capitalization and a host of other qualitative descriptors,' explains Ajoy. Meera recalls how the programme got branded Future Shock and why it was important to brand it. 'Titanians always galvanized themselves around a compelling theme. A clarion call like this worked because every one of them was invested in the future of this company and brand that they were so passionate about.'

The exercise was also meant to crowdsource ideas. The managers were divided into seven teams and their task was to come back with ideas for diversification that would suit a company like Titan. These couldn't simply be straws in the wind: each group had to cover market size, opportunity, specific products, the competition and prepare a five-year business plan. Of course, they were given time to do this, and each group was also appointed a mentor. Ravi Kant recalls, 'It was a fairly intense exercise, the teams were allocated funds for their research and given six months to come up with their ideas. At the end of this, each team had to make a presentation to a final jury which comprised members outside the company from industry and academia; it was like making a presentation to a private equity fund since you wanted someone to invest in your venture and you had to be convincing.'

As Meera recalls, 'All teams were [also appointed] a financial anchor. Because the teams were mandated to ensure that the new business ideas they came up with would meet the gross margin targets set for them to "qualify" to be a Future Shock business idea.'

Harish Bhat recalls the Future Shock exercise vividly. 'When Bhaskar first stood up to introduce Future Shock to some of us in the leadership team, the power of this incredible effort did not strike me immediately.' Harish was a member of the team mandated to reimagine Tanishq. As the team got into full flow, they found that the exercise opened up their minds, energized their thinking and led them into numerous interesting discussions about the future of the business. 'I still recall making part of the final presentation on the future of Tanishq at the HAL auditorium which is just off the old Airport Road in Bengaluru. We faced a volley of questions from the audience, the atmosphere was electric and we responded with alacrity and confidence,' says Harish.

Future Shock, says Harish, set in motion a very different kind of envisioning. 'Fifteen years later, I still carry in my wallet my name card for Future Shock, given to me on the date of the final presentation. I carry it because it constantly reminds me of the power of an extraordinary team effort that helped transform Titan.'

By the end of the programme, many ideas were thrown up, some of which Titan later explored and grew into businesses.

While Titan steered clear of suggestions for women's apparel, footwear, do-it-yourself furniture, design services and educational toys, it did eventually venture into eyewear, a mass-market jewellery brand (Gold Plus), fragrances and precision engineering. Those who came up with successful ideas were invited to be part of the business if it got going. 'From this exercise we picked up ideas which drew the greatest energy and passion and were also logical for the company. We had two dimensions: one set looked at new categories and businesses which were in the marketing or retail fields and then there were a set of ideas which were engineering-led. We didn't pursue the engineering ones because they didn't look attractive from the economic angle. We also wanted a good return on investment since we were coming from a weak business position and had set ourselves a goal of achieving high profits. That played a role in steering us towards more retail-led categories,' explains Ajoy.

Clear Vision

When Ajoy was vested with the task of piloting the eyewear business, his first line of action entailed visiting optical fairs, opticians, eyewear stores, looking at the supply-and-distribution chain, indeed the whole gamut of operations relating to the business. July 2005 saw Ajoy and his team make a presentation to the board. 'It was the first time I was attending a meeting where the chairman of the board [Mr Rameshram Mishra] was present. I was told that the eyewear business did not excite or enthuse him but he would give me 15–20 minutes since it was on the agenda. So there was a lot of pressure. After the presentation he said this was a great line of business and why didn't we approach the board earlier?' recalls Ajoy with a chuckle.

Eyewear was not entirely a novel idea; since 2003 Titan had been retailing sunglasses under the Fastrack brand, but the real business lay in prescription eyewear. They hit upon this insight when they started working with opticians as a channel of distribution, as well as visiting international optical and sunglasses fairs. Indeed, they discovered that the ratio of prescription eyewear to plain sunglasses was 80:20, not just in India, but internationally too. This insight was later validated through market research studies and sizing of the optical wear market in India. 'But I had to convince the internal team of its business potential because none of them wore glasses. Since I wear glasses, I could instinctively see the business potential. They saw prescription eyewear as a health issue and their argument was that we were not in that segment, we were more in the style segment,' says Ajoy. It took a lot of convincing on Ajoy's part to make his colleagues understand that wearing stylish spectacles was as much a style statement as anything else.

Ajoy's joy was doubled when, apart from getting an okay from the board, a Dalal Street big bull and longtime investor in Titan, Rakesh Jhunjhunwalla, who holds a substantial stake, told Bhaskar that eyewear was a *halwa* business – meaning, it would make a lot of money. 'He said there's a lot of money to be made in it and the margins are attractive, and he recounted his not-so-great experiences with opticians and stores,' recalls Ajoy.

The business was incubated in the watch division, where Harish Bhat had brought in Ronnie Talati from Fastrack to be in charge of the project. He was seconded by Biju Alexander, an early management trainee in Titan, who was moved full-time to this project. 'There were many debates as to what brand the business should operate under and whether at all the Titan name should be used. After many debates, it was decided to leverage the Titan brand name which stood for fashion and style and add "Eyeplus" to the name to prompt the category of prescription eyewear,' explains Ronnie.

Eyewear retailing at that time was largely unorganized and retailing practices left consumers feeling 'uncomfortable' at best. For instance, spectacle frames were kept hidden in drawers under the counter, denying customers a view of the entire range; unbranded frames were passed off as branded goods and pricing was arbitrary. When it came to lenses, pricing became even more opaque and customers never really knew whether they had been charged fairly. Titan Eyeplus entered the market using trust and transparency as its platform. It hired Pune-based Elephant Designs to create a design for its stores that had spectacle frames displayed in a browse-and-feel format with prices tagged on each product, a lesson picked up from watch retail. Titan Eyeplus opened its first store in Safina Plaza, Bangalore, in 2007 – the same facility where Titan had opened its very first store in 1987. Four stores sprang up in the incubation phase and the learnings from them helped shape the strategy for future expansion. Titan found that the browse-and-feel format was working well; having multiple brands was superior to stocking only Titan-branded eyewear. Once the eyewear business began to gain traction, it was spun off into a separate unit with Ravi Kant in charge.

Ravi Kant's move to eyewear in 2007 followed a successful stint in watches and in marketing Tanishq in West Asia. 'Eyewear was new to me, so it was virtually training on the job. I went around visiting opticians, looking at products, competition outlets, meeting ophthalmologists, lens specialists, et al., to get a good understanding of the business,' he says.

Bhaskar explains Titan's foray into seemingly unrelated businesses as an entry into categories that are largely unorganized and where the consumer is underserved. In an interview published in *BusinessLine* on 3 October 2013 at the launch of its Skinn range of fragrances in Mumbai, Bhaskar said, 'The idea is to unearth more and more underserved categories. The Indian middle-class today has access to hundreds of products, which is 20 times more than what they had 30 years back. People have the required disposable income. There are still many categories in India that are age-old and have no [big] manufacturers. They may not be a ₹2,000-crore market but we bring value. What is wrong in creating a ₹500-crore brand?'

Ravi Kant clarifies the point further. 'When you look at an unorganized market where there aren't too many big players, the opportunity to bring about change is much higher. Eyewear was a category where customer education made a lot of sense. A huge percentage of people are not even aware that they require vision correction.' There were just a few national chains of opticians when Titan started; the bulk of the market constituted unorganized players or mom-and-pop stores. 'When we got into this business, the unorganized market was as high as 80–85 per cent. It's difficult to judge but we think the share has come down to around 70 per cent,' says Ravi Kant. Titan changed many rules of the game in the eyewear industry, ranging from introducing the concept of 'browse, select, buy', with prices marked, in retail stores to transforming this category into a lifestyle accessory.

With Titan Eyeplus now on the go, all sourcing of spectacle frames was done mainly from China, an arrangement that still continues, while lenses were sourced locally from reputed brands such as Essilor. To train store staff, in January 2008 Titan set up the Titan Eyeplus Training Academy in Hosur with Sankara Nethralaya, the well-known Chennai-based eye hospital, as its knowledge and content partner for optometrists and store staff and for the eye-testing and dispensing processes. 'We enlisted qualified optometrists as well from the market, further trained them and put them through our own certification process. We also trained sales staff as eyewear consultants and technicians to fit lenses,' explains Ravi Kant. As of 2018, Titan Eyeplus has trained 2,500 optometrists and 4,000 store staff at its training centre.

While the optometrists Titan hired needed to have a minimum qualification of a diploma or a bachelor's degree in optometry, sales staff who go on to become eyewear consultants usually do not have a formal qualification. Rather, individuals with sales experience in the retail sector are hired and trained. Ravi points out that earlier, first-time users of spectacles would prefer to get their eyes tested by an ophthalmologist but now with good quality optometry being provided by organized chains such as Titan, customers visit good optical stores for a primary eye test and go to an ophthalmologist only if they have a medical problem.

Titan kicked off the business on a franchisee model which it had perfected with the watch experience. The stores had smartly turned out sales people, an in-store optometrist and eye-testing equipment. However, the going was not easy, admits Ravi Kant. The best locations meant higher rentals, and technically qualified staff came at a price. Clearly, the estimates had to be completely reworked. Investment on store interiors had to be pared down to improve the margins for franchisees; in order to do this, the stores called for remodelling.

Titan also had to battle the public perception of Titan Eyeplus as being expensive. Consumers were ready to spend more on shoes and shirts but less on eyewear and Titan was forced to introduce cheaper frames and lenses in order to cater to the price-conscious buyer. 'We also had to reorganize the stores depending on the catchment and profile of customers. A store on Bengaluru's MG Road will be different from stores in the suburbs. We did this repositioning, including a lot of communication, [based] on the affordability of the brand,' says Ravi Kant. Titan Eyeplus's specialized services, such as high-index lenses for those with a high degree of myopia, unique coating on the lenses for those spending long hours in front of a computer screen, lenses that could repel dust and water and so on, slowly began to gain traction with consumers.

Titan has always preferred to own all the elements of the value chain for all its businesses and it wasn't long before it decided to establish its own manufacturing facilities. The eyewear division set up its first lens-manufacturing facility in Chikkaballapur near Bengaluru in 2010 at a cost of ₹32 crore, using what it calls the latest 'free form technology' to grind the lenses. The technology predominantly used by most traditional Indian lensmakers is a grinding technology where the power is 'ground' physically onto the outer surface of the lens. Titan's lens factory uses a digital manufacturing process with computer-aided design and surfacing to create customized spectacle lenses. This gives users improved clarity of vision with greater contrast and provides for brighter and more intense colours. Today, 80 per cent of Titan's lens sales comes from its Titan branded lenses produced in-house and 20 per cent from the Essilor brand.

In 2017, Titan Eyeplus completed 10 years in the business; it started to rake in profits in 2015. Today it has a footprint of close to 500 retail outlets in 203 towns across the country, six million customers have shopped in these stores and the business has a turnover of over ₹500 crore a year. However, competition has intensified with existing, reputed opticians expanding their reach and venture-funded online stores now setting up physical stores and aggressively marketing their offerings with full-page ads in the newspapers, making unbelievable offers on frames and lenses. In 2015, Ravi Kant moved out of eyewear to return to head the watch business. Ronnie, who had meanwhile become the chief marketing officer of watches and accessories, replaced him as CEO at Titan Eyeplus, returning to the business he had helped incubate.

Ronnie is confident that Titan Eyeplus can hold its own in a competitive market. The division, he says, has four satellite lens-manufacturing units in Kolkata, Delhi, Mumbai and Bengaluru. 'This has enabled the eyewear business to offer faster delivery, even on the same day, to its customers in these regions, [a service] most competitors are unable to offer,' says Ronnie. Plans are afoot to set up similar units in Patna and Chennai. The main lab at Chikkaballapur can churn out 1,000 lenses a day while the smaller labs can produce 500.

Titan also recently invested over ₹30 crore to set up a frame-manufacturing unit, also at Chikkaballapur, with a capacity to make one million frames a year. 'This will allow us to substitute imports, bring down costs and, in conjunction with a recently set-up design studio, offer differentiated and high-quality products in the market. Commercial production of frames has already commenced and is expected to benefit the business greatly,' he explains. While the bulk of the eyewear business sales will come from its own brand of frames, the stores also stock top international branded frames such as Ray-Ban, Oakley, Carrera and Vogue, among others. With a well-established back end to support its growing chain of stores, Titan's eyewear business is poised for exponential growth.

A Scent of Success

One muggy morning in March 2011, Rajeshwari Srinivasan found herself in the vast and bustling flower market of Malleswaram, one of the traditional shopping districts of Bangalore, with a clutch of French perfumers. After they had soaked in the fragrances of the market, Rajeshwari walked them around the leafy locality, taking the motley group to smell the camphor in the temples, the fruits and vegetables in the market, and even getting them to experience travelling on a local bus and the metro. She took them to various nooks and corners of the city, including the Titan stores, as well as the watch and jewellery factories in Hosur. 'I think I made them walk around half of Bengaluru city. They had to soak in as much as they could of India,' recalls Rajeshwari, a TAS officer, with a chuckle.

The launch of Titan's Skinn brand of perfumes was still many months away but Rajeshwari, who spearheaded the fragrances business project, and her team wanted the French perfumers to engage with the sights and smells of the country before they delved into their exotic art to come up with the right perfumes for the Indian market. 'We wanted them to understand the smells of India because we were very clear that the perfumes they created would have to linger through the day and have the ability to rise above the ambient smells of India. They also had to understand how people used perfumes, and how they were being retailed,' explains a team member. Of course, understanding the market required many trips to India, and many of those in the French group returned to India again and again to get a sense of it.

This was not Titan's first brush with perfumes; it had had a brief dalliance with perfumes earlier when it launched Evolve, also created in France, in the West-Asian markets in 2006. The product proved to be successful and Titan used all the learnings from it to create a new business model that eventually developed into Skinn. While Evolve was successful in the competitive and crowded West-Asian market, Titan subsequently shelved its plan of bringing it to India or taking it to other markets as it decided to focus and grow its core business of watches and jewellery.

When Rajeshwari joined Titan in 2008 from Indian Hotels, another Tata company, Titan was looking at new businesses to explore. Bhaskar suggested reopening the fragrances segment given Titan's earlier positive experience. 'At the new business development group, incubated by Bhaskar, we were looking at multiple projects and the fragrance category was one of the stronger projects with a clear value proposition for premium customers who were beginning to spend a larger discretionary income share on "looking and feeling good",' she explains. Having the managing director himself backing the idea gave her great energy and sense of purpose, she says.

The business model had to reflect the tastes of customers who were high fragrance-users in their daily lives, right from *dhoop* and *agarbatti* to flowers. 'The fragrances had to stand out,' says Srikanth Sudarsanam, a member of Rajeshwari's team. Consequently, two years (2009–2011) were dedicated to intense qualitative market research. The tastes of customers were gauged on the basis of research involving 2,000 customers across India. The research clearly revealed that Indian customers wanted to buy French-created or inspired perfumes because of the romance associated with them. The research team rigorously did its homework: it looked at the stories behind the best perfumes, studied various methods to make perfumes, looked at the main manufacturing centres and the key makers of perfumes and the multiple layers that play a role in taking a perfume to the market. Many management trainees who interned at Titan were tasked with different aspects of the research, with a core team anchoring the project. The team also looked at the supply chain and visited perfume bottle and cap-manufacturing plants across India and China, supplying some of the world's best perfumeries.

Properly armed with information, Titan then approached two of the best perfumery houses in France, Givaudan and Firmenich. Bernardo Cauvin of Givaudan and Luc Berriet of Firmenich, fragrance development directors for Asia and the Pacific, had a long and rich history of developing fine French perfumes for the world's best brands. Then there was also Delphine Roussel at Givaudan. These experts were involved with Skinn's odyssey right from the beginning. They were given a written brief so they would have a clear understanding of the kind of customers that Titan Skinn would appeal to and the perfumes that Titan wanted. They were given eight months' time to develop the options for the perfumes, and were expected to supply by early 2012.

Luc remembers his interactions with Titan vividly. 'We were contacted directly by Titan for this project. They had specifically asked to work directly with the French perfumers. They came to visit our development centre at Grasse in the south of

France. It was a special relationship from the start. They had hundreds of questions about the perfume business,' recalls Luc. 'I could see that Titan wanted to bring the world's best to Indian consumers at affordable prices. Now that was an eye-opener as they wanted to get the finest in terms of quality and creation. That was very important for me. And, that's something I took back with me when I returned to Paris to work on the project and with the perfumers.'

Skinn's Indian team also made several immersion trips to France and China. As Gaurav Khanna, then marketing manager of the fragrances division recalls, 'We were in Grasse visiting rose and lavender fields during peak season. It was a surreal experience.' Besides, the perfumes were created by talented international experts such as Olivier Pescheaux (Boss Selection, Vanderbildt and Higher Dior), Harry Fremont (Mont Blanc, Victoria's Secret and Ralph Lauren), Michel Girard (Burberry, Ferragamo and Lacoste), Fabrice Pellegrin (Paco Rabanne, Insense and Givenchy), Nadege Le Garlantezec (Jasmin, Junaid For Perfumes and Ego Facto) and Alberto Morillas (Giorgio Armani, Estée Lauder, Lancôme and Versace). 'We were working with really top-class perfumers. They realized quickly that what would work would be specially customized perfumes and they needed to be modern and international, with a strong smell code, a technical term used by perfumers to reflect a strong smell versus a mild smell code. They created 250 to 300 versions of the perfumes they were working on. 'We narrowed it down to three families of smells [day wear, evening wear, sporty wear for men and women] and each perfume house created about 50 versions in each of the families. There were altogether about 300 variants and we chose six variants from among those – three for women and three for men,' says Jayshankar Menon, the sales head.

The research had shown that there were several male and female archetypes, each desiring a unique fragrance. As Skinn's fragrance development manager Malavika Kalauny points out, they realized early on that Indian consumers verbalized perfumes as fresh, floral or spicy. 'Clearly our work was cut out as we needed to offer three clear, customized perfume variants; creating one standard perfume was not going to be enough. Indian consumers love to test and buy in multiples and offering a cache of perfumes made sense,' explains Gaurav. Established international brands do a single launch of a variant and a perfume at a time but Titan felt that it needed to appeal to different people and multiple preferences and had to offer a bouquet of perfumes at one time.

Meanwhile, Bhaskar was of the view that any business needed to be armed with financial resources and dedicated manpower right from when the project was launched in order to maximize the sense of ownership and drive. So, Ronnie Talati came on board to lead and mentor the team, and the chief operating officer of the watch business, H.G. Raghunath, came in as chief sponsor. Between them they had enough experience to guide the team. The team too had grown, with each member wearing multiple hats. With support pouring in from other departments such as design, visual merchandizing, commercial, IT, regulatory, and individual employees putting up their hands, saying, 'This is my skill set, how can I contribute to this project', the perfumes project took on a strong sense of shared responsibility.

The top brass comprising Bhaskar, Venkataraman, Ravi Kant, Harish Bhat and Subbu Subramaniam, the chief financial officer, were regularly updated. The Skinn exercise gave the company significant insights not just into perfumes or how to put a business together but also to the fact that 'at the end of the day, everyone is a customer [–] for themselves or for gifting. We all learnt the business together,' explains Rajeshwari. For instance, hundreds of employees volunteered to 'smell' and help shortlist the perfumes that worked; they came tirelessly in batches of 25 to do this.

The branding exercise the team embarked on involved multiple approaches on whether it should be a solo brand or one with multiple brand names. But it also needed the credibility and brand name of Titan to resonate with the consumer. The team pondered over how and where to bring in the Titan name. At the end of one such 'smelling day', Bhaskar simply said, 'Let's name it Titan Skin, which is both intimate and sensuous and also the part of the body where you actually use the perfume.' Intimate and sensual were also two aspirational qualities that any great perfume should have. So Skinn it was christened, the additional 'n' was added to allow for brand legal rights as 'skin' is a generic word. All the right ingredients were in place for a sweet-smelling project.

In March 2012, Rajeshwari, who by then had been formally appointed head of the fragrances business, made a very compelling presentation on Skinn to Titan's board of directors at the annual board meeting in Goa, and got a favourable response. The team got the approval to go ahead with the project. Orders were placed on the perfumery houses, giving a lead time of six to eight months for the supplies to arrive in India. The perfumes also went through intense skin tests. 'There are about 16 tests that the perfumes are put through,' says D.S. Lokesh, part of the sourcing team. Pharmacological clearances had to be obtained before the 'Made in France' label could be put on the bottles. And the bottles themselves had to be designed; in the fragrances business they are as important as the perfumes. The first few designs for Skinn were developed in-house by designer Neil Foley, Michael's brother, who was also with Titan.

The countdown to D-Day had begun. However, to the team's chagrin they discovered that making the perfumes in France was the easy part. Bringing them to India was tougher. One of the challenges, they realized, is that only specific freight carriers were allowed to carry alcoholic cargo – including perfumes – and that also required specific documentation. After the perfumes were finally cleared through customs and the products were placed at all the large department stores, the World of Titan stores and large specialist stores across the country, Titan readied for the launch.

Skinn was launched on the auspicious day of Ganesh Chaturthi in September 2013 with a grand party at the Taj Mahal Hotel which was attended by the glitterati of Mumbai as well as the top Tata honchos. The fragrance of Skinn had finally arrived. It was also time for Rajeshwari to move on to another role in Titan and the baton passed on from her to Kalpana Rangamani. In 2015, the fragrances business and the team were moved into a newly-formed business incubation division led by Ajoy Chawla. It was created to look at scaling up new categories like Skinn and to also incubate new categories as future growth drivers for the company. Although the fragrances business had great potential, it still needed nurturing, focus, dedicated people and sustained marketing investments if it was to achieve the threshold scale.

Under Kalpana's leadership and Ajoy's mentoring, the business grew from about ₹6 crore (2014–15) to an estimated ₹90 crore in MRP terms (at retail prices) in four years. Investments were made in terms of presence in 2,000-plus points of sale, 29 exclusive kiosks in malls and airports and promoters (also referred to as beauty assistants) in close to 350 points of sale, besides initiating innovative marketing communication across television, print and digital media.

Skinn became the first brand in India to run a television advertisement entirely in French – to both emphasize its French parentage and rise above the noise of the hundreds of ads that consumers are exposed to at all times. Its product portfolio has grown from 12 stock keeping units (SKUs) across six fragrances to 40 across 13 fragrances. Skinn was also the first fragrance brand to do trials with airline flyers by tying up with Jet Airways and Vistara where the air hostesses would hand over small vials of the perfume to flyers. All these efforts have seen Skinn emerge as the number one brand by value in highly competitive channels like Shopper's Stop, Lifestyle and Central, in each of which close to 70 international brands compete for customers' attention, according to Kalpana. The team's long-term aspiration is to make it a ₹500 crore business serving 4 to 5 million customers.

Weaving New Ideas

Titan has always been known to be an intrapreneurial organization with several new business ideas, products, retail formats, sub-brands and so on having emerged from its middle management and then supported by top management. 'This has been in the DNA of Titan and its culture of openness, its non-hierarchical structure, its innovation has been a great enabler,' says Ajoy.

To leverage the strong sense of innovation in the company, sometime in 2012–13, when there was a lot of buzz around Bengaluru as a start-up capital, Titan came up with a programme called 'Ignitor'. It was a programme to open up the process of ideation on new businesses that Titan could get into. Anyone in the organization could form teams and send in business ideas with a write-up and a PowerPoint presentation on the opportunity they received and why Titan should take it up. 'We got over 750 entries and this was followed up by a structured process of shortlisting and then asking the shortlisted teams to come up with a more structured body of thought and present it to an external jury in a couple of months. This got further pruned to three final ideas which seemed to be interesting opportunities, were a fit for Titan and could have a good business model,' recalls Ajoy. These three teams then got a chance to work on building a more refined approach with research and even budgets for prototyping and were presented to an internal panel which then decided what would get piloted. 'Overall, it got us some new business opportunities and people felt energized and more engaged as they were able to express their ideas; they saw this as their way of co-creating Titan's future,' he says. In other words, it gave them a sense of ownership.

One of the ideas that emerged from the Ignitor exercise was for Titan to enter sarees as a business. With that in focus, Titan embarked on yet another interesting brand journey with Taneira sarees, all natural and handwoven, curated from the diverse weaving and craft clusters across India. According to multiple sources, including a study by retail consultants KSA Technopak on the ethnic wear market, special-occasion women's wear featuring sarees, lehengas and other ethnic wear is worth ₹25,000 crore and is growing in healthy double digits. This category has seen a lot of buzz in recent years, driven by a pride-in-India trend, a renewed sense of Indian-ness, a celebration of Indian culture, Bollywood themed weddings and an overall move towards branded products. These factors are inspiring people to buy sarees, even if they spend more time inside the cupboard than draped on individuals, says Ajoy. Taneira sources its selection from over 55 handloom clusters either directly from master weavers and cooperative societies or through designers and aggregators. It also has its own designers working on the project both for sarees as well as blouses and lehengas.

Titan is sticking to its principle of looking at what it calls 'underserved categories' and building a national brand out of it. 'Not just in branded, lifestyle retail, we also seem to do well in categories that are not very well penetrated or are unorganized or where customers are underserved,' says Ajoy. In this, the company enjoys certain natural advantages. 'We can leverage the same customer group as for Tanishq and Raga. The second is size. Now we are a large company, so any category we enter should create a ₹500–₹1,000-crore opportunity in the future. This is our aspiration and also a prerequisite,' says Ajoy. Taneira could well be the next Tanishq for Titan.

It's Not Just About Business: The Titan Township and School

Long before corporate social responsibility became a buzzword, it was part of the Tata Group's philosophy and action plan. When the Titan factory was dedicated in March 1988, J.R.D. asked to meet with Xerxes and Anil Manchanda. There was no specified agenda and so they had no idea what to expect when they arrived at Bombay House, but they were sure it would be a quick visit. J.R.D., Anil recalls, heaped praise on the factory, which he said was the best, bar none, in the Tata Group and better than most he had ever visited in India or abroad. They had not yet stopped beaming when J.R.D., speaking softly as he always did, asked what Titan was doing for the community around the factory. Surprised, Xerxes said that Titan could plan a medical centre for employees and a scholarship scheme for students from the neighbourhood. 'For the first and last time in my 20 years with Tatas, I saw a flash of anger in Mr Tata's eyes. He said, still softly, "Why are we talking about peanuts? You know what we are doing elsewhere. Let's do something meaningful in Hosur like building a first-rate school and a hospital for the people who see this magnificent island of prosperity we have put up in their midst with no direct benefit for them",' recalls Anil.

It was true. Although Titan employees enjoyed comforts at their 'five-star' factory, they went back home every evening to poor, rented housing. Spurred on by J.R.D.'s words, Xerxes felt the creation of a well-designed township would admirably address the gap while creating an asset which, at worst, would increase in value over time. Titan acquired 110 acres of land 8 km from the Hosur factory and developed the basic infrastructure such as the levelling and grading of the land, the provision of roads, the drainage and the laying of power and sewage lines. Employees had to acquire the plots and arrange for the construction of their homes

The township's master plan was designed by Charles Correa, and it was inaugurated by Chairman Ratan Tata in 1992. Residents of the township were polled for their preference of school board affiliation and medium of instruction. The concern was that the language used in the classrooms might not be the language used at the dining table. But parents would have none of it. They opted for English, recalls Vikram. Why English? – and pat came the response, 'software, Bill Gates'. English and CBSE it came to be. In 2001, the school, meant for all children in the vicinity, formally opened its doors with a nursery and primary classes before it was formally established as a higher secondary school. Xerxes formed a taskforce of eminent educationists to develop the vision, mission and values for the school. At his last public appearance at a school function, where Bhaskar and other senior Titan officials were present, Xerxes declared that 'the school has far exceeded the expectations of the founders and if there are a few things that make me happy towards the end of my life, one of them is the Titan School.' Just days later, on 26 June 2016, Xerxes passed away in a hospital in Bengaluru. He was 79. He had lived to see his dream fulfilled.

EPILOGUE

Titan is today a large company in the consumer goods space and immensely profitable. It's a retailing behemoth with 1,480 exclusive stores in 276 cities and towns spanning over 1.9 million-square feet of retail space in 2018. This is a quantum leap from the situation it found itself in when Xerxes Desai retired in 2002 and Bhaskar took over, saddled with debt from the European fiasco and the Tanishq jewellery business not yet having turned around. It was probably not a legacy Xerxes would have wanted to leave behind.

While the losses from the European business had to be written off over the next few years, Tanishq prospered to become perhaps the first national jewellery retail chain. While Titan made a strategic withdrawal from Europe, leaving Xerxes's dream unfulfilled, in later years it carefully explored markets surrounding India, in the East as well as in West Asia, and today exports its watches to over 25 countries. In the Bhaskar era, it was no more about plunging headlong into businesses without carefully curated pilot projects. However, Xerxes did leave behind a 'no guts, no glory' spirit of experimental adventuring which was recalibrated by Bhaskar.

What Titan's Tanishq business is today owes itself to Xerxes's vision His gumption and determination helped the company stay the course. Despite the many naysayers, Xerxes stood his ground on the belief that the business had long-term potential. There were many in the Tata Group who said that jewellery was not Titan's core competence as it was a watch company. But as Xerxes says in the book *Tata Log* by Harish Bhat, 'I ask you, if the Tatas had focused only on their core competence, wouldn't we have remained a textiles and trading group for the past century?' It was a powerful argument.

The culture that Xerxes created in Titan continues to stand the company in good stead – a culture of openness and innovation, with a high sense of aesthetics and fastidious attention to detail. The DNA engendered by Xerxes of refinement and quality runs deep in Titan. A people's man who led the company with an easy hand, Xerxes's Titan attracted top-drawer professionals who worked with passion and dedication. He was able to inspire people, synthesize their talent and bring out their best. Most of Titan's senior management team comprises those who joined the company at inception or soon after in the late 1980s and have stayed on, deeply steeped in the Titan culture.

Xerxes inherited J.R.D. Tata's 'management by affection' philosophy and the uncanny ability to pick the right people for the job, mirrored in his selection of Jacob Kurian when the Tanishq business was in a crisis, and also in his passing the baton on to Bhaskar Bhat who steered the company out of trouble and into profitability.

While Titan has captured the market for watches in the affordable segment, scaling up the brand to become a premium player in league with Swiss brands might be a difficult proposition. Titan has been associated for too long as a maker of reasonably priced watches with the bulk of its watches in the mid-market segment. Tata Group Chairman Emeritus Ratan Tata recognizes that challenge when he says it would be easier if Titan created a new brand for the premium space (watches costing ₹15,000–₹20,000 and upward) or even bought a brand in the premium segment than for Titan to move some of its products into the premium space. Titan has, indeed, made some of the moves Ratan Tata advocates. It bought Swiss brand Favre Leuba to break into the premium space though the brand itself is perhaps not quite in the same league as the top Swiss brands. Favre Leuba continues with its Swiss heritage and is made in Switzerland and has its own marketing team based there.

Apart from the challenge of moving into the luxury/premium category, there is the fact that most young people today no longer wear watches; in the age of the smartphone they prefer to consult their mobiles. Also, mobile and tech giants such as Samsung, Apple and Google have invaded the watch space with wearable technology and smart watches that not only tell time, but also track location, provide health parameters, advocate exercise and do a hundred other things; the more premium of these offerings are pretty much mini life-organizers.

Titan has recognized these challenges and continues to re-craft its strategy for the watch business with investments in technology. Its foray into smartwatches in an increasingly connected world will be a key growth driver. A few years ago, Titan tied up with Hewlett Packard to launch Juxt, a premium watch that connects by Bluetooth to a cell phone, and receives alerts on its dial. Wearables is another category that is very promising for Titan; its Fastrack Reflex fitness band, priced a shade under ₹2,000, has sold over 300,000 units as of March 2018. The future is clearly new technology and Titan has a pipeline of futuristic products ranging from smart belts and wallets that integrate new technologies and new platforms like NFC (near field communications) and payments whereby payments can be made through a digital wallet in a watch.

Titan's jewellery business today dwarfs the watch business (₹13,036 crore to ₹2,126 crore in 2017–18) though, as Bhaskar points out, selling at least 15 million watches a year, the watch business touches many more customers than the jewellery business does. Titan has also made an online play by acquiring CaratLane, an online jewellery retailer, two years ago. Will CaratLane establish a new paradigm in jewellery retailing in India? Only time will tell, but clearly Titan is pursuing both brick and mortar and online retail, or omni channel, as a way of the future. It has tied up with Flipkart where one can buy spectacle frames or sunglasses frames online and walk into any of the over 500 Titan Eyeplus stores to have the lenses fitted.

Titan's other businesses – eyewear at ₹415 crore (in 2017–18) and accessories, fragrances and sarees, are still in their infancy, but growing rapidly. Those who track Titan closely say it needs another big idea, like Tanishq, to pitchfork the company into its next growth phase. They say Titan needs to leverage what it does best – design, aesthetics, branding and marketing – and build a blockbuster brand in the next category it enters.

In its 30-year journey, Titan has reinvented itself many times over, picked itself up and reconfigured its business as well. There's no doubt it will be ready for the next challenge. And, at least in Titan's case, it wouldn't be trite to say, time will tell.

ACKNOWLEDGEMENTS

This book was made possible thanks to the support of many people. I am grateful to the following in particular: Mukund Padmanabhan, formerly editor of *BusinessLine* and now editor of *The Hindu*, who gave me the go-ahead to write; the current editor of *BusinessLine,* R. Srinivasan, for his support; Ratan Tata for his perspective on Titan and to Tata Sons chairman, N. Chandrasekaran, for writing the foreword; Bhaskar Bhat, the managing director of Titan Company Ltd, who, in the midst of his busy schedule, found time to give me valuable inputs and also fix key appointments for me; the late Xerxes Desai, with whom I spent many hours talking about the company he helped create; Anil Manchanda, whose prodigious memory helped fill in all the little details concerning the early years of Titan.

Thanks are due to the entire Titan team without whose stories there would be no book. Momita Das helped set up many meetings in the early stages of my interviews and Sirish Chandrashekar tirelessly supplied me with the required figures and pictures. Harish Bhat, a writer himself, was kind enough to be a sounding board at times when I was stuck and also read the chapters. I'm grateful to the senior management team at Titan who willingly gave of their time, and for the many hours spared by S. Ravi Kant, Ronnie Talati, C.K. Venkataraman, Ajoy Chawla, Rajeshwari Srinivasan, Revathi Kant, Subbu Subramanian and other Titanians for this book.

Thanks also to a whole bunch of former Titanians, retired or having moved on, who are still passionate about Titan and gave me key insights: Minoo Mody, Khushroo Kapadia, Ravi Kant (Sr), Vibha Paul Rishi, H.G. Raghunath, Vikram Rajaram, Jacob Kurian, Bijou Kurien, M.S. Shantharam, B.G. Dwarakanath, Manoj Chakravarti, Shridhar Subramanian, Vasant Nangia, S. Deenadayalan. Meera Harish understood the spirit of the book well and gave me delightful anecdotes and insights from the life of Titan. Thanks too to Sanjay Ranawade of the jewellery factory and R. Rajagopalan of the watches factory for the time they spent with me. And I must express my gratitude to a whole host of Titanians I spoke to at the corporate office as well as at the factories. I may not have been able to quote everybody in the book; nevertheless the conversations I had with them were enormously useful in completing this book.

Many from outside the Titan network, but deeply involved in its advertising and design, also spoke at length to me. Thank you Roda Mehta, Ashok Sarath, Rajiv Menon, Sanjiv Khamgaonkar, Radhakrishnan Nair, Michael Foley, Piyush Pandey and R. Balki. Thanks too to C. Sivakumar who gave me a retailer's perspective.

Thanks to K. Gnanadesikan, chairman of Titan Company Ltd, for having made the time to speak to me. And also to former Titan chairmen and former Tamil Nadu bureaucrats, who offered their insights: Iravatham Mahadevan, Debendranath Sarangi, Shaktikanta Das and C.V. Sankar. Others such as D. Shivakumar, Vinita Bali, Rishikesha Krishnan, Malavika Harita, Ramanujam Sridhar and Harish Devarajan offered valuable insights from an outsider's perspective.

Thanks, of course, to Hachette India's managing director, Thomas Abraham, who spotted a book when I proposed the idea, and to Poulomi Chatterjee, editor-in-chief, Hachette India, who whacked my journalism-infused writing into book shape. I'm grateful to my editor, Sandhya Rao, who painstakingly went through several drafts and to Hachette's Ansila Thomas for giving the book a final read.

I thank my *BusinessLine* colleagues, B. Baskar, who helped me with the transcripts, and Anand Kalyanaraman, who readily gave me support on data. And, of course, a big thanks to my wife, Aruna, who patiently put up with all my procrastinations on various fronts during the course of my writing this book.